EVERYDAY LIFE IN ELIZABETHAN ENGLAND

EVERYDAY LIFE IN ELIZABETHAN ENGLAND

Text by
DAVID MOUNTFIELD

Liber

Contents

© Editions Minerva, S.A., Genève, 1978
Printer, industria gráfica sa   Provenza, 388, 5.ª   Barcelona
Depósito legal B. 22318-1978
Printed in Spain

1. GOLDEN AGE

THE ENGLISH RENAISSANCE

It would be possible to paint a picture of life in Elizabethan England as cruel, grim and depressing. Life expectation was short, infant mortality high, social security almost non-existent, disease uncomprehended and starvation quite possible. A shockingly large proportion of people were unemployed and compelled to support themselves by begging or robbery. The distribution of wealth was grossly unfair; one good meal at court could cost the equivalent of ten servants' wages for a year. A few people were brutally killed for their religious beliefs; a few were lynched as witches. Irish peasants were robbed and murdered; the African slave trade began.

These things should not be forgotten. But they do not destroy the impression that the late 16th century was England's Golden Age. Like every Golden Age, it had its black impurities. Life was not all honey and roses in Pericles' Athens, nor in the Medicis' Florence, nor in Jefferson's America. And life in Elizabethan England was, for some people, as miserable as life can be. For others it was —and they knew it—a heroic age.

This Golden Age was very short, as golden ages always are. Strictly, it could be confined to a mere twenty years—the last two decades of the 16th century. Nearly all the cultural adornments of the reign of Elizabeth (1558-1603), of which Shakespeare's plays are the greatest, come from the second half of the reign. They were carried over into the reign of James I (1603-25), but by 1600 that curious spirit of sophisticated melancholy which may perhaps be regarded, at least in its exaggerated form, as a symptom of cultural decline was sapping the spirit of creativity, while a trace of coarseness, apparent even (for example) in furniture design, was growing more pronounced.

It would be rash to attempt to account in precise terms for the blossoming of the English Renaissance in the late 16th century. But the existence of certain favourable conditions is clear enough.

England had recently emerged from a prolonged period of upheaval, economic and religious. Elizabeth's father, Henry VIII (1509-47), for reasons of state and personal prejudice, had overthrown the religious establishment which had lasted nearly a thousand years. He had abolished the power of the Pope and set up a national Church headed by the monarch. He had further dissolved all the great religious houses, distributing their extensive estates among those of his subjects willing and able to pay. But he had not permitted any radical change in church worship or doctrine. He remained a Catholic, though not a Roman Catholic. However, towards the end of his life he was increasingly surrounded by people sympathetic to the doctrines of Luther and the reformers, and he appointed Protestants as the guardians of his young son, who succeeded him as Edward VI (1547-53).

In Edward's brief reign, England became thoroughly Protestant. The Prayer Book of 1552 went so far as to expunge words like "priest" and "altar" from its pages as smacking of popery. But Edward was followed by his Catholic elder half-sister, Mary Tudor (1553-58). Mary's mother had been Spanish and she saw her mission in life clearly: to return England to the Roman Church. To help her do so, she married King Philip II of Spain, which was unpopular, and she executed

Left, detail from a contemporary painting about the life of a distinguished Elizabethan, Sir Henry Unton.
Below, silver medal (1588) with the head of Queen Elizabeth I.

5

Above, Richmond Palace, as it looked in the time of Elizabeth I. Right, detail from a tapestry showing the area surrounding Hampton Court.

about 300 Protestant heretics, which was even more unpopular, especially as many of the victims were ordinary folk. Executing bishops or lords was one thing, but to execute tradesmen and their wives for their religious beliefs seemed needlessly harsh.

But Mary's reign too was short, and in 1558 the young Elizabeth came to the throne. One of her first priorities was to bring the religious pendulum, which has swung so wildly to and fro since her father's time, to a peaceful stop in a reasonably central position. In fact, the Elizabethan religious settlement was a good deal further Left than the Queen would have liked, but it was accepted by the great majority and it proved enduring. Later in the reign, Spanish-inspired Catholic plots provoked some cruel treatment of a few innocent individuals, while at the other extreme, Puritans launched their sometimes narrow-minded criticisms of society; but on the whole the Elizabethan religious settlement was a success.

Economic and political unrest was also dying down. From the 1530s to the 1550s there had been several popular risings, none of them perhaps particularly dangerous, though nonetheless alarming to the government. They were caused by a mixture of grievances, over new farming practices which caused unemployment, over taxes and "arbitrary government", besides various local complaints. Elizabeth faced a number of conspiracies but only one serious revolt, and that was confined to the North of England, at this time still a wild and savage place and only doubtfully under government control. From the 1580s, the growing threat from Spain helped to consolidate the spirit of patriotism.

In Elizabeth's reign, the English embarked upon their great maritime adventures, which were to take their ships, their merchants and eventually their soldiers and governors to most parts of the world. But the empire lay in the future: the first American colony was not founded until 1607. There was every opportunity for maritime enterprise, without the responsibility of colonial commitments.

The expansion of English sea power, which was partly a result of, as well as an encouragement to, the growing sense of nationhood, might not have taken place but for the changing relationship with France. The claim to French lands, indeed the French crown (a claim never withdrawn until the 19th century), had been the continuing theme of medieval foreign policy. But by the middle of the 15th century, when the 100 Years' War finally petered out, the English had lost all their possessions in France except Calais (which was lost in the reign of Mary Tudor). Thereafter, wiser and more "modern" heads wore the crown, and there

Facing, a contemporary allegory of the rich man and the poor man. Bottom, another contemporary engraving, illustrating the arrogance of an ambitious courtier: one of the characters is wearing breeches of Italian velvet, and the other of traditional English cloth.

were no more long and wasting wars with France. Occasional sorties there were; certainly a monarch of Henry VIII's cut could not resist the temptation of a crack at the traditional enemy, but his cooler father, Henry VII, always recognised that trade was more profitable than war, and his projects against the French were merely designed to top up the royal coffers: parliament voted money for the campaign, then the French king paid Henry a fat bribe not to attack him.

Thus the English stumbled upon the policy which was to bring them power and greatness: they acknowledged that they lived on an island, and behaved accordingly. They avoided continental entanglements and strove for control of the seas, and this policy was not completely abandoned until the 20th century.

A generation after Shakespeare's death, the fissures in English society were to split wide open and full-scale civil war was the result. Already there were rumblings of the troubles ahead.

During Elizabeth's reign, the English people (always excluding the large but voiceless masses of the poor) were prospering. Exactly who was getting richer, and why, are questions which have exercised historians greatly in recent years: the status of the gentry in Elizabethan times—rising or falling—has been one of the most discussed problems of English historiography since the publication in 1941 of a famous article by R.H. Tawney, "The Rise of the Gentry". But there was a lot of new wealth about, some of it plundered from the monasteries. And although individual members of the gentry may not have been "rising" at all, the standard of living for most people was going up—not only for those with large estates but also for yeoman-farmers (typically, small freeholders), for merchants, craftsmen and professional men.

In this environment, great reserves of national vitality were released. The sheer zest with which Shakespeare, or any of a dozen or more lesser poets, manipulated the language was characteristic of the age. The avarice with which wealth was pursued was another, less attractive aspect of this same energy and zest for life.

That halfway house between the medieval and the modern was an exhilarating habitation. The old shibboleths, the mental tramlines of the past were vanishing, while the new neuroses had not taken hold. Rank superstition mingled with world-

8

ly cynicism, feudal attitudes were found in capitalist enterprises: such conflicts and contrasts, while causing many odd, even disastrous, mistakes, had a liberating effect on the mind.

It may seem odd, especially to a citizen of Florence or Rome, to speak of the Renaissance at the very end of the 16th century. Certainly, although England was behind the times, it would be quite wrong to suppose that the culture of the Renaissance was unknown there until the reign of Elizabeth. Her father, Henry VIII, would have been outraged at the suggestion that he was any less cultivated a "Renaissance Prince" than his contemporary, François I. He was, after all, himself a composer of music (though not, according to modern critics, a very distinguished one). But in Henry's reign the Renaissance in England had still been mainly restricted to the society of the royal court and a few centers of learning such as Oxford and Cambridge. In Elizabeth's time, the Renaissance had become "popular". Shakespeare's plays were not written primarily for a tiny, informed coterie, but for ordinary people—merchants, craftsmen and apprentices—the same people who purchased and sang the popular ballads and the stories of ancient Greece and Rome. Shakespeare set several of his finest plays in classical times which, to him and his contemporaries, were far more immediate than they seem to us.

Soldiers of the Elizabethan age.

"GLORIANA"

Shakespeare's England, we say, thinking of the greatest Englishman of the time. Others, and certainly all contemporaries (many of whom had never heard of Shakespeare) would call it the Queen's England, Elizabethan England. The Queen personified her country and her age in a vivid, direct way: she was even more "Elizabethan" than Queen Victoria was "Victorian", and that golden light that seems to illumine the age glows most brightly around the figure of Elizabeth herself. Almost alone among the major figures of English history, she has no serious detractors. Her faults—vanity, faithlessness, obstinacy—are undeniable, and not all trifling. But few historians of the age have quite succeeded in escaping from her spell. Like them, her courtiers and poets flattered her, but it was not hard for them to fashion the extravagant conceits of the cult of "Gloriana", for they were, all of them, more than half bewitched.

Yet there was nothing dreamy or superficially romantic about the Queen. Her virtues, like her ancestry (a fact of which she loved to boast) were thoroughly English and practical. She was, first and foremost, a practical politician, surely the most able politician who has ever sat on the English throne. At her most wilful, she never lost sight of realities. Even towards the end of her life, when she appeared an almost sinister figure—her face expressionless for fear of cracking the thick cosmetic layers which endeavoured to disguise the advance of time—she never became the neurotic

tyrant that her father had been in his last years.

As a child, she had needed a cool head to survive amidst the political fluctuations of the time. On one occasion she had spent a period as a prisoner in the Tower and narrowly evaded a charge of treason. This dangerous childhood taught her caution, and though there were times when she carried caution too far, it was a failing on the right side, and one that was not common among dynastic monarchs. That apart, she often seemed to have the elusive political gift of choosing the right policy almost by instinct, always knowing how far she could go and when she should retreat. She had the faults of a successful politician also: she was not straightforward, and her public conduct was sometimes nothing better than deceitful, though the ends might have been held to justify deceitful means.

Elegant and stately, she was also fiery and quick-tempered, as her red hair and dark eyes hinted. Otherwise, her portraits are not always helpful. They often look almost like icons, or representations of a religious idol. Poets too turned her into something unhuman. She had beautiful hands, of which she was proud, but she was also capable, in a rage, of using them to box someone's ears. She could reprimand the Polish ambassador in Latin for a furious ten minutes, then turn to her court with some deprecatory, tongue-in-cheek remark about her rustiness in that language.

Occasional rages notwithstanding, Elizabeth was by nature tolerant and kind. Although she failed to establish a "middle way" in religion, she was on the side of moderation in enforcing the settlement. Personally, she had no wish to "make windows into men's souls," as she put it, and religious persecution in England, even after Elizabeth had been excommunicated by the Pope (who thus invited her Catholic subjects to commit treason) was milder than in many other countries. The Queen's dislike of war was, like her predecessors', based on the clear realisation that it was likely to be economically unprofitable and socially disruptive; but she also disliked it because it was cruel, a view that would not have found much sympathy with her ancestors.

Elizabeth was a woman of parts, genuinely intellectual and well educated. Her fluency in Latin dated from her 16th year, when her tutor reported that "she talks French and Latin as well as she does English" (though her Greek was

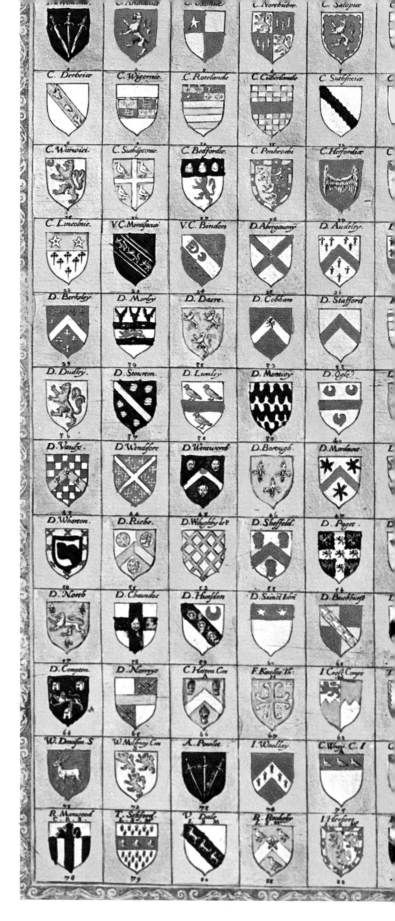

Facing, the shields of the Elizabethan courtiers. Below, the Court of Wards and Liveries in session, under the chairmanship of Sir William Cecil.

only "moderate"). She also had a smattering of German and Spanish. This linguistic ability was politically important. England's experience of queens regnant had been brief and unhappy; moreover, in the 16th century, women were definitely considered the weaker sex. Lord Burghley once reprimanded an ambassador for troubling the Queen with a matter not fit for women's ears. Elizabeth therefore had to struggle, at the beginning of the reign, to keep the strings of government firmly in her own hands. Her knowledge of languages meant that she could deal directly with foreign ambassadors and keep foreign policy under her personal control. (Her closest and longest-serving minister, Burghley, happened to be poor at languages, or so he said.)

Her favourite amusements were music and dancing. During one of her numerous abortive courtships, she met her suitor boating on the river and entertained him on the lute. She could also play the virginals; indeed, a surviving 16th-century instrument is popularly believed to have been the Queen's. There is also a 16th-century painting of some elegant people dancing in which one couple is traditionally identified as Elizabeth and her favourite, Robert Dudley, earl of Leicester.

When Elizabeth came to the throne, England seemed little more than a humble appendage of Spain. By the time she died, it could combat Spain on equal terms. For that, the talents of the Queen and her well-chosen ministers could take much credit.

Above all, she was an inspiration to her people; to humble folk as well as poets. Her speech to her soldiers at Tilbury, when England was in danger of a Spanish invasion, is as well-known and as stirring as any of the patriotic speeches Shakespeare put into the mouths of the characters in his historical plays. (Of course, we do not know how accurately she was reported, but that does not alter the general impression.) No less remarkable was her "golden speech", in the 44th year of her reign, when she addressed members of the House of Commons for what many of those present, perhaps including herself, must have realised was likely to be the last time. "Though God hath raised me high", she told them, "yet this I count the glory of my crown, that I have reigned with your loves", and "though you have had, and may have, many mightier and wiser princes sitting in this seat, yet you never had, nor shall have, any that will love you better".

There can be no doubt that the Queen's love

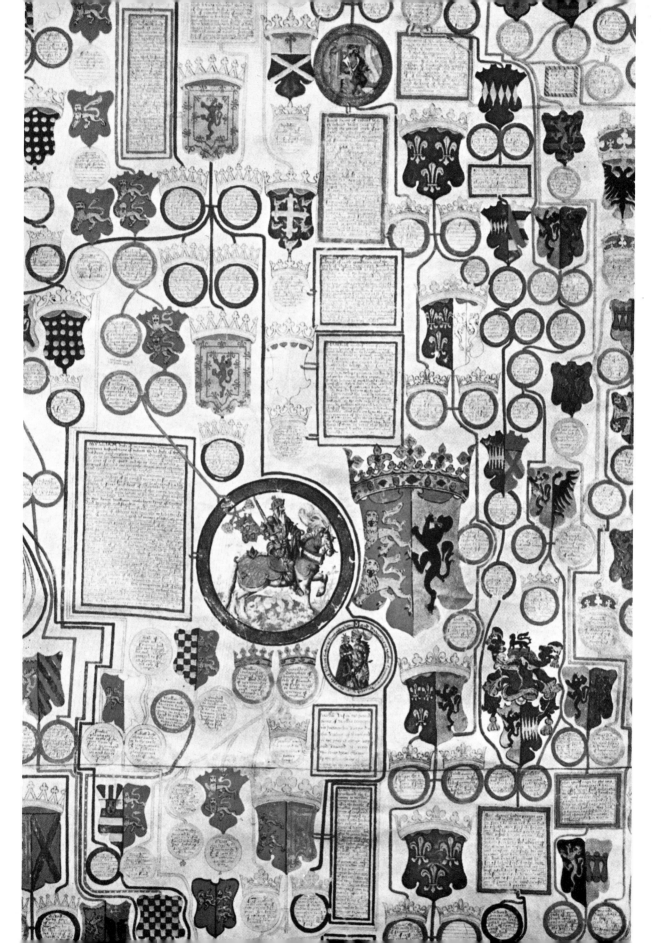

for her subjects was heartily reciprocated. She was identified, personally as well as symbolically, with the fortunes of the nation. She was frequently visible, at any rate in the south-east, on her journeys, and not a remote figure. Loyal addresses to a ruler are by their nature laudatory, but the note of sincere affection in the Commons' addresses to Queen Elizabeth is clear enough. The story is often quoted of a pamphleteer who had opposed Elizabeth's projected marriage to a French prince, an audacity for which he lost a hand. As his right hand was chopped off, he raised his hat with his left and loudly shouted "God Save the Queen".

Ordinary fishermen and their wives, from the south-east coast.

COURT AND COUNTRY

The monarch was indisputably the governor of the kingdom in the 16th century. The doctrine of the "divine right" of kings to rule, which was to land the Stuart kings in such trouble, was tacitly accepted by nearly everyone in the reign of Elizabeth. The Stuarts (James I and Charles I) proclaimed "divine right" as a threat and a weapon. Elizabeth would never have made such a mistake. Towards the end of her reign, the Commons became incensed at the granting of monopolies (which gave the grantee exclusive rights to sell a particular article). The Queen, who was as keen to uphold the royal prerogative as James I, recognised the strength of the opposition to monopolies, and withdrew, conveying the impression, not that she had been forced to do so, but that she had graciously consented to the wishes of the Commons out of sheer benignity.

The function of parliament was still very limited. It had been used as the constitutional means of bringing about the Reformation, the greatest constitutional change the country had ever known, and this had given it greater power and prestige. Statute law was recognised as the highest law, but statute law was law passed by "the king in Parliament" and the most important part of that combination was not parliament but the king.

Government revolved around the monarch. Members of the Privy Council, secretaries of state and other ministers were the servants of the monarch, appointed by him and dismissed by him at will.

The royal court was merely the immediate environment of the monarch. Elizabeth was a constant traveller in summer, so the court was frequently on the move. There were of course institutions of government, such as parliament, permanently established in the capital, but the court remained the centre of law and administration.

It was also the fount of favour, the bright magnet that attracted ambitious young gentlemen from distant shires—or indeed, elderly gentlemen in search of a state pension.

The court displayed the striking contrasts of the age, elegance side by side with coarseness, sophistication mingling with simple-mindedness. Etiquette was not so highly developed as at Louis XV's Versailles, but it was extensive and complicated nonetheless. The Queen's public movements were surrounded by ceremony and ritual, much of it completely non-functional. Laying the dining table was a lengthy ceremony: even the man who brought in the table cloth was preceded by an attendant. Yet when all was done, the food was carried away to the Queen's private apartments.

14

The notables of the day: they are symbolized by the wife of the Lord Mayor of London, here shown in a procession.

Yet Elizabeth could be informal. She would also ride pillion on horseback, hanging on the rider's belt.

The court was large. Excluding visitors, it numbered roughly 1,000, of whom about half were government officials. There was a vast hierarchy of officials and servants, their duties carefully graded. Everyday maintenance and supply was the province of the steward, while the lord chamberlain, a man necessarily of encyclopedic knowledge, supervised the ceremonial affairs of the court—its public aspect. He had an enviable command of patronage. Open-air functions, including the hunting parties enjoyed by Elizabeth and adored by James I, and the incessant journeys of the Queen, were the domain of the master of the horse.

On her journeys, the Queen was in the public eye and could be approached by comparatively humble subjects without great difficulty. Unlike Versailles, for instance, the English court was not insulated from the rest of society: court gossip could be picked up in St. Paul's cathedral and soon reached the ears of anyone interested. The court was also, in spite of the ceremonial, less lavish. Elizabeth, who was always desperately short of money (in her later years she was compelled to the desperate resort of selling Crown land), made severe economies in court expenditure.

Needless to say, the court, as such, was not popular. The courtier was regarded with contempt (when is he not?), and Hamlet's opinion of Osric ("this waterfly") probably represents the robust citizen's idea of a courtier. The hostility was no doubt a case of sour grapes. The court was the place to get on, the place where a gifted and handsome young man from an obscure and impoverished family of gentry could rise to a position of unrivalled prestige and enormous riches. And though not many could do as well as Sir Walter Raleigh, the opportunities for advancement were still numerous. After all, the Tudor ancestors of the Queen had been minor landowners in Wales who made a success at court in the early 15th century. It was still not too difficult to get a foot in the door, although if you were not so fortunate as to be born into a noble family, it was necessary to find a patron who would introduce you.

The court of Elizabeth was said by a patriotic commentator (who had possibly never been there) to be "one of the most renowned and magnificent in Europe".

Able herself, Elizabeth liked to have gifted people around her. In that respect she was unlike her successor, James I, who though equally clever was more didactic by temperament and was content for his young men to be merely gorgeous and charming.

2. THE FAMILY

FAMILY PRIDE

The family was one the strongest sinews that bound society together. In many respects, indeed, the family was a microcosm of the state. It was run on rather similar lines, with the head of the family as "monarch" arranging marriage alliances with neighbouring families to augment family estates much as kingdoms allied themselves for mutual benefit. Family pride was a kind of small-scale patriotism: it was both a reflection of and a stimulus to the pride of the nation itself.

Family pride was not just a glorification of ancestors, though that was certainly part of it. It was less conservative and more forward-looking than such feelings usually are today. A family history compiled in 1593 portrays the characters of contemporary members and describes how their property was, by one means or another, amalgamated over the course of time, thus raising the family from the status of yeomen to that of country gentlemen. It was compiled, its author said, for the benefit of his descendants. They should learn thereby something of their predecessors and, more particularly, of the complicated rights and titles of land involved in the estate, which would enable them better to contest any future disputes over property. This mixture of antiquarian interest and legal shrewdness is highly characteristic of the times.

Dynastic security was ensured by the possession of land and the principle of primogeniture. Though hard luck on younger sons compelled to make their own way in the world, primogeniture prevented estates being split up by death. As at any other time, estates could be lost through ill fortune or maladministration, but on the whole the larger the property, the more stable the family. Many great Elizabethan landed families have remained in possession down to the present. Further down the social scale there was more mobility: as wealth and property decrease, sharp fluctuations in family fortunes become more common.

The preoccupation with wardship is one sign of the contemporary devotion to the idea of a continuing line. Sir Walter Devereux, fearing he would not live to bring up his children, urged the Queen to take his son as her ward, otherwise the boy would grow up in a manner "far unworthy of his calling". Children were often sent to live in households where they might acquire advantages not available at home.

It would be misleading to speak of snobbery in Elizabethan England if the word is used in the sense that it acquired in the 19th century. Nevertheless, in that age, as in most others, people were highly conscious of their social status, their place in the hierarchy. According to Thomas Nashe's account of London (1593), "The rich disdain the poor. The courtier the citizen. The citizen the country man. One occupation disdaineth another. The merchant the retailer. The retailer the craftsman. The better sort of craftsman the baser. The shoemaker the cobbler. The cobbler the carman."

Gentility was a quality to be striven for, and if possessed, to be jealously guarded against slights or encroachments. Squabbles over precedence at court and furious local rivalries in the countryside, provoked by efforts to assert gentility or denigrate it in others, remind us that this was a "high-stomached" age (the stomach was associated with pride).

It was not, in fact, too difficult to become a gentleman. Shakespeare managed it although he was only an actor, a profession little higher than that of the highest rank of servant. However, Shakespeare's father had been at one time a fairly substantial citizen of Stratford and owned some property

Top left, engraving of the rather well-stocked family of an Elizabethan aristocrat. Bottom, the family at dinner. Below, the family of the third Earl of Windsor.

in the town. According to Sir Thomas Smith, writing about twelve years before Shakespeare's birth, "as for gentlemen, they be made good cheap in England. For whosoever studieth the laws of the realm, who studieth in the universities, who professeth liberal sciences, and to be short, who live idly and without manual labour, and will bear the (expense) of a gentleman, he shall be called master, for that is the title which men give to esquires and other gentlemen, and shall be taken for a gentleman... And (if need be) a king of heralds shall also give him for money arms, newly made and invented, the title whereof shall pretend to have been found by the said herald in perusing and viewing of old registers..."

THE HOUSEHOLD

The household of a nobleman or country gentleman included a remarkably large number of people, sometimes over one hundred. Size was a rough indication of social status: the greater the gentleman, the more numerous were his attendants. But besides servants, and the immediate family, there were likely to be many other dependents and relatives, including young married couples who had not yet set up home for themselves (like the daughter and son-in-law who lived with that famous victim of the Reformation, Thomas More), as well as, often, young friends or relations sent there by friends or relatives for the sake of a better education in gentlemanly (or ladylike) behaviour.

Indisputably, the head of the household was the husband and father. Wives were expected to be obedient to their husbands, and all the preachers who expounded on marriage, a favourite subject for sermons, started off by emphasising the absolute necessity of wifely obedience. The happiness of everyone depended on the character of the head of the household. If he happened to be by nature a mean and cruel tyrant, there was not much to be done about it, as long as he kept within the bounds of the law. But such behaviour would have aroused the contempt of neighbours and acquaintances, and must have been rare.

A man had obligations to his home no less than to the Church and the State. The head of a household, though he had many privileges, also had serious duties and responsibilities. He was responsible for the good name of the family, and had to protect the reputation of his wife and children at all costs. The deepest scorn was reserved for the man who failed to uphold the reputation of his wife or allowed her to become the victim of that scourge of society—gossip.

Another obligation, which could have an appreciable effect on family fortunes, was hospitality to guests—and, on occasion, to strangers. The amount of food consumed, or at least ordered, by large households in Elizabethan times was prodigious. Beef and mutton particularly were consumed in huge quantities, although it is possible that some of the few surviving figures may be misleading, representing, possibly, the operations of a dishonest steward.

But hospitality had to be generous, that was expected. A visit from the Queen herself was enormously costly, and those who were so privileged as to receive a royal visit must sometimes have contemplated the prospect with mixed feelings, to say the least. The Queen did a great deal of visiting because, among other reasons, it saved the court a great deal of money, an advantage which the parsimonious monarch was quick to take. It is said that her favourite, the Earl of Leicester, died

up to his neck in debts as a result of his lavish entertainment of the royal court. These hazards, however, affected only a few households.

At any level of society, family life was a serious business. Gentlemen absent from their homes worried about what was happening in their absence. They were inveterate letter-writers, in spite of the slow and chancy means of delivering mail, and inundated their wives or their stewards with the minutest details of what they ought to be doing in the orchard, or the buttery, or the nursery. Children away from home, perhaps at university or the inns of court, were expected to write home regularly. But parents were not satisfied with that. They also sought reports from the boy's tutor and asked anyone travelling to the place where their son resided to call on him and bring news of his welfare. Sometimes, the carriers who took their ponderous wagons from town to town were asked to undertake this kind of mission, and were even paid a fee for doing so.

A household in the country was largely self-supporting. There would be a greater number of articles purchased rather than made at home than in earlier times but, basically, household management had changed very little from the kind of system seen in a medieval manor. Apart from one or two luxuries, all the food was grown on the home farm. Bread was baked in the bakery, beer brewed in the brewery. Most of the clothes were made at home, and so were items like candles. The 16th-century household was a beehive of industrial activity.

The head of the household was mainly concerned with questions of long-term policy, such as the marriages of his children or the acquisition (or sale) or land. He presided twice daily at family prayers, unless he employed a private chaplain, and led the household to church on Sunday. (Elizabeth's subjects may have been more agnostic than either their grandparents or their grandchildren, but they were still a religious people.) During the week, the country gentleman probably spent most of the day in the fields. The everyday running of the household was the business of his wife.

Inside some stately homes: Benthal Hall; Levens, Westmorland; Broughton Castle; Ockwells, Berkshire.

The description "clean-fingered", applied to a woman, was by no means a term of approval. Wives were expected to get their hands dirty, in spite of the crowds of servants available. So numerous and complicated were the tasks performed in the household which today require only a visit to the supermarket, that the lady of the house had to know many skills. She had dozens of jobs to do which have long since become redundant.

A contemporary writer, Thomas Tusser, listed some of the activities of the ideal country wife in a relatively ordinary household. She governs the household, seeing that every servant is well occupied and well behaved: her concern for their welfare even extends to stipulating when they should change their own clothes. She rises early in the morning and gets all the servants working at their appointed tasks. She supervises the serving of their meals, keeps an eye on important household processes like brewing, baking and cheese-making. She keeps an eye out for vagrants and stray dogs on the scrounge, she collects feathers for stuffing pillows and makes her own candles (thrift was the greatest virtue of a housekeeper, especially in Puritan households). The evening meal is not served until she has made sure the farm animals are safely housed (in a larger house that would probably not be her responsibility), that the laundry is gathered in, so that it will not be stolen by wandering beggars, and that the dairy is safely locked.

One might think she had little time for leisure. But ladies went hunting and hawking or, like Lady Hoby who did not like blood sports, played bowls. It was a full life.

THE DAILY ROUND

The hours kept by the people of Elizabeth's time were very different from the hours kept by their descendants. In their day, "midday" really was the middle of the day. The average working day, for those engaged in agriculture, was from 05.00 to 17.00 hours. As there was no artificial lighting more efficient than candles, the utmost use had to be made of natural light; hence early rising and early bedtime.

There were exceptions to the early rising rule. Then as now, people tended to get up later in the city than in the country. This was already a cause of unfavourable comment by writers on social

mores, though the accusations levelled against fashionable people in London that they stayed in bed until 11 or 12 o'clock were no doubt much exaggerated.

In a respectable household, the day began with a sign of what would be a recurrent preoccupation until night fell again—prayers. Not only were prayers said twice a day, but the Bible was often read at meal times (sometimes by one of the children) and at other quiet periods. A well-to-do lady in Yorkshire, who kept a diary for several years around 1600, found time for private prayer and meditation in her chamber, and for talks with the domestic chaplain. This clergyman would read to her and her maids while they did their work in the house. Nor was her religion entirely inward looking. She would visit the poor living round about and instruct them in religion.

By 08.00, when the modern office worker is just opening his eyes, the people in the Elizabethan market were closing up their stalls. Work on the farms stopped for a simple meal. At the manor house, tutors were already arriving for daily lessons. In one household, the daughters studied French between 7 and 8. At 9 the dancing master arrived; at 10 came the singing master and another musician who taught them to play the virginals. Nor was this the extent of their musical education: lessons on the lute and viol began at 4 in the afternoon. For much of the rest of the day, the girls were occupied in various kinds of needlework and embroidery (a particular skill of the English since Anglo-Saxon times), which they would offer for their mother's critical inspection in the long gallery.

Working at embroidery with her maids was also an occupation that took up much of the Yorkshire lady's day. Otherwise, she was busy supervising the many household tasks of her servants, or performing them herself. In her household, the midday meal was a major event. Dishes had to be scraped or wiped clean, napkins folded, knives scoured, cloths laid and stools put in place by the table. The various staff—butlers, pantlers, servers—had to be prepared.

For humbler folk, the midday meal was a simpler affair. Workers were able to eat their food, take a nap after it, and still be back at work in a field or stables before 2 o'clock. At that time, even the most lavish dinners were finishing. The taverns were emptying and, on the south bank of the Thames at London, the playhouses and bearpits

were opening.

Those who were fortunate enough not to have to work in the afternoon might go walking about their estates or gardens. They might go fishing or play some outdoor game like bowls, or they might pay or receive a visit. There was not much reading, not for relaxation or entertainment anyway. After the Bible, the most popular book was the formidable Protestant propagandist work known as Foxe's *Book of Martyrs*.

By about 5 work was ceasing, the schools were closing, and the evening meal was being prepared: for the humbler classes, it was the main meal of the day. In midwinter, it was already quite dark at that hour, and people were guided through the streets with flaming torches. The only lights in the house were candles, and the glimmer of the fire. Even for the hardest-worked, there was a little leisure time in the evening, when cards or some other indoor game might be played. But by about 8 o'clock, they were on their way to bed.

In larger houses, the day was often prolonged. At court, dancing, masques and other revels might keep the gallant throng (and, of course, their attendants) up till the small hours. But that was exceptional. Even the rich normally kept to an early bedtime. By midnight there were few Englishmen who had not yet said their nightly prayers and climbed into their beds. After that, the night belonged to the watchmen, patrolling the streets with their lamps and calling out the hours.

Three hundred years ago, winter was more than a discomfort, it was a real hardship for many people who were unable to keep themselves warm or properly fed. But it had some compensations. Since the days were short, so were the hours of work—at any rate by comparison with summer. Some of the old craft guilds had laid down that no work at all should be done in January, when the light was so poor that delicate craftsmanship was possible for only the briefest time.

Apart from the leisure enforced by darkness, Sunday was a day of rest and, although church attendance was compulsory and some activities were banned as unseemly for the sabbath, it offered the one substantial respite from the week's work. For since the Reformation, holidays were fewer: saints' days were no longer regarded as holy. However, some religious festivals were still held, and there were feasts and celebrations at harvest time and on May Day.

3. WOMEN

WOMAN'S PLACE

England is a paradise for women, a prison for servants and a hell for horses, ran a contemporary saying. Like most such proverbs, it is more memorable for its neatness than its accuracy, but any foreign visitors did testify to the comparative freedom of women in England. The Duke of Württemburg remarked in 1602 that there was more liberty for women than in any other country. Another traveller commented on the number of females present in any random crowd: Englishwomen, he observed, like to be in on everything. They even went unaccompanied into taverns and theatres. In several epilogues to his plays Shakespeare appeals particularly to the women in the audience, as though their judgment was of primary importance.

Contrary to the custom of other nations, a patriotic Englishman asserted, the English "give the higher place and way" to women, but by this he meant merely that men stand aside for women, assist them on to their horses, and so on.

A Dutch diplomat was perhaps more perceptive about the freedom of women. He agreed that married women possessed an unusual degree of liberty, though he compared the English situation with that in Spain, never exactly in the forefront of female emancipation, rather than that in his own, more liberal country, where indeed (he thought) unmarried girls, unlike wives, were freer than they were in England.

And the wife, though she had the management of the household and appeared to have her own way most of the time, was ultimately in the power of her husband. He could not kill her, of course, but quite respectable men saw nothing very reprehensible in beating their wives. A prominent judge once gave his daughter a brutal flogging because she demurred at his choice for her husband. There was no question but that women were subservient to men.

Elizabeth's subjects regarded man and woman as two quite different creatures. It was widely believed that male children were formed on the right side of the womb, female children on the left. To a great extent, woman was the opposite

Throughout the whole of society—in the countryside, among the rich and the not-so-rich, and at family gatherings—one finds the eternal pair of lovers.

of man, with contrary qualities. Man was hot and hard, woman cool and soft (another interesting biological theory was that the sex of a child depended on the temperature in the uterus: if sufficiently warm, the child would be a boy). From warmth comes courage; from coolness comes timidity: hence the greater boldness of man, the comparative weakness, both mental and physical, of woman.

Woman was expected to be beautiful. This is, of course, contrary to the usual case among animals, where the male is the more splendid partner. Shakespeare's contemporaries tended to think, like many others, that beauty was Nature's gift to woman in compensation for her deprivation of brains, which belonged to man. However, there was no doubt that woman *was* the more beautiful, and this was a great virtue, one to be cherished. It was customary to endow women with the quality of beauty whatever their actual appearance, and thus the lavish courtship of the elderly and ugly Queen Elizabeth by a dashing young gallant like the Earl of Essex was slightly less grotesque to contemporaries than it seems to us.

Though not impartial to the charms of youth, the Elizabethans admired a mature woman. On the other hand, with their sharp and sad awareness of passing time, they were inclined to dwell on the transitory nature of physical beauty, and to advise their female readers to concentrate on the beauty within.

Although there was a strong dose of anti-feminism in much of the popular literature, woman also had her supporters. William Austin, in an essay in praise of women published in 1637, put forward views to which the most radical feminists of our own time could scarcely object. Woman, he said, is different from man in a physical sense only: "for she has the same reasonable soul, and in that there are neither he's nor she's, neither excellence nor superiority. She has the same soul, the same mind, the same understanding..." (Quoted C. Camden *The Elizabethan Woman*, Houston 1952, page 30). Their reputation for deceitfulness, said women's defenders, is because they learned to lie in the service of their husband's reputation.

Heroic women were also popular; especially, perhaps, heroically chaste women like Lucretia, whose rape by Tarquin is the subject of one of Shakespeare's two long narrative poems. This predilection was as familiar to the 14th century

as to the 16th or 17th.

In general, though, the virtues for which women were praised were exactly those that arouse the ire of emancipationists: besides chastity and modesty, humility, moderation, prudence, thrift, evenness of temper, etc. These, at any rate, were what men wanted;but there is a contrast between literature and behaviour. It would be wrong to regard the women of Shakespeare's England as oppressed, and conforming meekly to masculine will. Nothing could be further from the truth. For plentiful examples of independence, wisdom, and strong character, indeed wilfulness, in women, it is necessary to look no farther than Shakespeare himself. Portia, in *The Merchant of Venice*, is the strongest personality in the play, and no one accustomed to women as feebly compliant creatures could have created those unlovable sisters, Goneril and Regan.

Some feminine types, and moments in the life of a society lady: gambling, and going out with her husband.

The Countess of Pembroke, one of the most brilliant women of the period.

ANTI-FEMINISM

One difficulty in judging the status of women in Elizabethan England is that almost all the written evidence comes from men. There are a few exceptions, though a name like "Mary Tattlewell" is obviously a *nom de plume* and might even disguise another male writer (on the other hand, possibly some women writers were hidden behind the names of men). Still, there can be no doubt about the genuineness of Jane Anger who printed *Protection for Women* in 1589.

The Elizabethans were not uncommon in taking the attitude that women, however beautiful, virtuous, or even wealthy they might be, were essentially, as far as men were concerned, a necessary evil. Such a principle had been set down, as Robert Greene put it, by philosophers whose sayings have been held as oracles. The humorous, or not so humorous, disparagement of women was not unique to the English Renaissance, but it was a marked feature of popular literature. Possibly, the coincidental presence of so many female rulers in what was assumed to be a man's world had something to do with it.

A fervent believer in the total incapacity of women to rule was John Knox, Scotland's Calvin, who in his notorious pamphlet *The First Blast of the Trumpet against the Monstrous Regiment of Women* (1558) delivered his verdict that for a woman to rule over men was as sensible as a blind man leading the sighted. Knox's fury was directed at the numerous Catholic queens of the time; the accession of Elizabeth, the Protestant heroine, rather spoiled his case and compelled him to make a—characteristically ungracious—exception of Elizabeth from the "Monstrous Regiment".

Some preachers were even more radical in their anti-feminism, and denied that women had souls.

The belief that the origin of the word "woman" was "woe to man" was a popular one among the satirists. Derogatory comments on women from classical writers were eagerly disinterred, and so was Boccaccio's remark that God sent curses upon man, the last and worst of which was woman. A common figure of popular mythology in the 16th century (and earlier) was the "shrew"—the bossy, nagging, ill-tempered wife. Everyone knows of the severe penalties in the Middle Ages for "gossips"—those women (they seem to have been always women) who indulged in malicious talk (we should not underestimate the potential evil of gossip in an age when there was no more reliable method of spreading news, and when cross words quickly led to violence). Women, it was said, talked too much and could not be trusted with secrets; they were dissemblers, who would say anything in order to have their own way (those who made ·this criticism failed to observe that such were their only means of getting their way).

27

Facing, bridal procession. Bottom, a dowry being weighed.

MARRIAGE AND DIVORCE

"Of all actions of a man's life, his marriage does least concern other people", wrote one of Shakespeare's contemporaries, "yet of all actions of our life "tis most meddled with by other people". The married state was regarded as normal and desirable. It was ordained by God, and in spite of the Protestant tendency to interpret marriage as a contract rather than a holy sacrament, a stable family life based on marriage was encouraged by Church, State and most of the writers who dwelt on the subject. Various reasons were given for marriage, usually the male advantages only. The commonest were, first, to produce children, second, to provide satisfaction for lust (although one authority advised even husbands to take their wives not in a spirit of physical desire but in consciousness of the desirability of conception), and third, to provide comradeship. There were others, variously recommended.

The unmarried woman was to be pitied, and so, to a lesser extent, was the unmarried man. But there were defenders of permanent virginity in women (how could there not be, with a virgin queen on the throne) and, in greater numbers, of bachelorhood. The main male criticism of marriage was the same as it is now: that marriage restricts freedom. Anti-feminist writers found many other aspects to criticise, one cynic going so far as to remark that only two good things happened in a marriage—the wedding feast and the wife's funeral.

There was no lack of romantic love in life and literature, but romance had little to do with marriage. "Romantic" was virtually a synonym for "foolish", and the "love" to be found in marriage could amost have been equally accurately described as "duty". The husband expressed his love for his wife by protecting her and supporting her. It was necessary to make a very careful choice of matrimonial partner, not only because future happiness depended on it but because posterity depended on it no less—the main point of marriage being to beget heirs. Marriage was not to be entered into lightly, and the utmost caution was urged upon prospective bridegrooms. Pity the man who, after too speedy and casual a courtship, discovers—too late!— that his wife's beautiful golden hair is in fact a skilfully fashioned wig.

Physical beauty, although a desirable quality, was regarded by the "marriage-guidance counsel-

lors" of the day with distinct ambivalence. They felt it was a two-edged sword, and might bring more trouble than satisfaction. "Take her not for her outward person", said one of them, "but her inward perfection". Everyone agreed that virtue was more important than beauty. Whether they actually married accordingly is less certain. Virtue was less easily judged. Robert Cleaver, in a book published in 1598, listed six characteristics which the prospective husband should consider in a girl he was contemplating marrying. First came her reputation, second her appearance, third what she had to say (and whether she knew when to keep silent), fourth how she dressed, fifth the company she kept, and sixth her education.

Wealth was, of course, another desirable quality in a wife, and so was breeding, although marriages were expected to take place between people of the same social status. Young men were advised not to marry out of their degree, though some did. Marriages of convenience were the rule, and there must have been many examples of a headstrong and ambitious father compelling his unfortunate daughter to wed a man selected by himself. Yet forced marriages were treated with disapproval: *Miseries of Enforced Marriages* was the title of a play performed in 1607. Parents were not expected to marry off their children against their will, although a girl who married without her father's consent was committing a much worse sin.

Girls married young, almost as soon as they were able to bear children. Not only did this, it was thought, give them the best chance of produc-

ing a family (infant mortality was high), but at such an age they were still flexible and could be moulded by their husband. Shakespeare's Juliet was fourteen, and this seems to have been a normal age for marriage, although there was some opposition to such young brides. Vives, an author belonging to the early 16th century, said it was dangerous for 14-year-olds to bear children, and recommended 18 as the earliest desirable age for marriage. Husbands were older, but a gross disparity in age was frowned on (possibly because it was not uncommon).

It is often said that children matured earlier in the 16th century, but this is doubtful (it may have been a true statement three or four generations ago, however).

There was some prejudice against widows. They were not regarded as ideal wifely material, and some men held the opinion that widows should not take second husbands. This, like so much other earnest advice on the subject of marriage, seems to have been widely disregarded. We often hear of widows marrying again before the one-year mourning period, which was considered the respectable minimum, was over. The famous Bess of Hardwick certainly found no difficulty in terminating her widowhood speedily on three occasions. Her considerable wealth more than compensated for her previous experience and, indeed, for personal characteristics unattractive in a wife.

Though widows might inherit wealth and brides came with a dowry, wives, for all practical purposes, owned no property. Legally, it all belonged to their husbands, who could do what they liked with it.

There is in the popular literature a great deal of advice to men on choosing wives, but little to women on how to judge a prospective husband. Women, of course, had little choice in the matter, and most of the advice that was provided for them was concerned with the ways in which they might make themselves agreeable to their husbands. However, a wife's behaviour was held to reflect her husband's, and if she misbehaved he attracted the blame. A cuckolded husband was an object of contempt.

Marriages could be invalidated by ecclesiastical declaration, and if those involved were sufficiently powerful, this was done without much trouble. Queen Elizabeth more than once insisted on the clandestine marriage of one of her court ladies being annulled.

There were a number reasons for annulment of marriage. If some gross deceit had been practised in order to bring the marriage about, that would serve as cause to end it. And there were certain prohibitions, sometimes infringed uncaringly or even accidentally, which could later serve the same purpose. Henry VIII had sought divorce from his first wife, Catherine of Aragon, on the grounds that she was the widow of his brother, and that was a perfectly sound reason for divorce. What made Henry's case dubious was that a special papal dispensation had been secured to permit his marriage to Catherine in the first place.

It was far from certain that adultery was sufficient cause for divorce, though it was sometimes considered so. Altogether, divorce was far from easy and, in fact, it was very rare. Yet there was some contemporary anxiety about the stability of the institution of marriage. Laws were passed to protect it on several occasions (once in the reign of Henry VIII).

Below, a schoolmaster teaching his pupils to read.

4. CHILDREN AND EDUCATION

ATTITUDES TO CHILDHOOD

Visitors to art galleries often remark on the fact that in Renaissance paintings, children are represented not as children but merely as miniature adults. It is a good example of the hand reproducing the message of the mind rather than the eye; for in the Renaissance children were indeed treated as though they were small adults. In his commemorative life of the gallant courtier and poet Sir Philip Sidney (who, mortally wounded at the battle of Zutphen, is said to have refused the offer of a drink of water on the grounds that an ordinary soldier lying wounded nearby needed it more than he), Fulke Greville wrote, "I lived with him and knew him from a child, yet I never knew him other than a man". This was a compliment: children were inferior men, more ignorant, weaker and less reliable. The sooner they became adults the better, was the general feeling. Hence the pictures of children dressed incongruously exactly like their parents, and maintaining the same expression of seriousness.

Having little notion of "progress" or "evolution", Elizabeth's subjects did not conceive of children growing up, slowly and steadily, into adulthood. Shakespeare, in a famous passage, described the seven ages of man, from infancy to senility; but these seven ages were not so much a steady development as separate layers, rather like the "degrees" of society. Thus in education, there were no subjects regarded as particularly appropriate, or inappropriate, to a child of a certain age. Education started with the same subjects as it ended with, the only difference being that, the younger the child the simpler and more basic the lesson: as he grew older, he repeated the same study but with more complications introduced.

Life in Elizabethan England was hard; the standard of living which we take for granted would have been literally inconceivable 400 years ago in spite of certain luxuries which seem fabulous to us (a poor family, for example, might dine regularly on salmon). Hardship was to be expected, and no one supposed that children ought to be protected from the harsh conditions they would have to endure as adults. The sooner the youngsters learned how rough life could be, the better they would be able to cope with it. Parents were warned not to spoil their children by too much pampering.

This rather grim view of childhood was reinforced by Puritan prejudices. The infant, wrote one Puritan in 1612, is but a brute in the shape of a man. His body is conceived in an act of lust—the stigma of original sin—an act so vile that mothers are reluctant to explain it to their offspring. Man has no cause to boast of his birth, which caused pain and danger to his mother and brought him into a world of troubles which he appropriately greeted with floods of tears.

Nor does the situation improve greatly when the infant becomes a youth. "What is a youth", asks the same writer, "but an untamed beast?" His behaviour is clumsy and foolish, he does not understand good advice when it is given, he is interested, like a monkey, only in worthless toys and trifles. The state of youth is altogether so undesirable that it is "not worth describing".

Much as one might like to be a prosperous country gentleman, or a courtier of Queen Elizabeth I, one cannot but feel that to be the *child* of such a person would be most unenjoyable.

However, this dreary and oppressive picture needs some correction. Of course mothers delighted in their children as do mothers of any race or time. People were not immune to the more attractive

sweeten labours, but they make misfortunes more bitter. They increase the cares of like, but they mitigate the remembrance of death". (Bacon, *Essays*, qu. Wilson *op cit* p. 50). Bacon went on to speculate on the importance of children as witnesses for posterity (for Elizabethan Englishmen were no less concerned about their posthumous reputations than the ancient Romans). He suggests that the noblest works of creation have come from childless men, who strove to pass on their mental images when they had failed to recreate their physical images. This hypothesis seems rather dubious. Perhaps it owes something to Bacon's own failure to achieve fatherhood.

manifestations of childhood and, in spite of the general reliance on corporal punishment, toys and treats were not unknown. One amiable uncle, eager to teach his nephew to read, found he had spent twenty times as much on sugar plums as on hornbooks.

A happy picture of childhood is presented in a conversation between a mother and a nurse about a baby (published 1605), in which there is much warmth and charm, as well as much good sense. John Earle, writing about 1628, also provides a more amiable picture of the nursery, although the sweets which the parents offer their child are treacherously intended to lure him into swallowing a draught of bitter medicine. However, mothers still resort to this subterfuge.

"The joys of parents are secret", wrote Francis Bacon, "and so are their griefs and fears... Children

Facing, a wooden alphabet used in Elizabethan schools. Right, inside the Grammar School of Stratford-on-Avon. Bottom, cover of a grammar book.

CHILD LABOUR

Children being but miniature adults, though more troublesome, it was a natural desire to make them useful as soon as possible. Children had always been accustomed from an early age to help their parents make a living, and to this day there are parts of the country where, for example, the school absentee rate rises at harvest time.

Poor children who became the responsibility of the parish were placed in the care of foster mothers, who taught them some craft at which they could earn a few pennies a week. Older children were apprenticed to a trade. This meant that their master fed and housed them as well as teaching them his trade, in return for their labour. Obviously, much depended on the character of the individual master: he might be a heartless tyrant, or he might be a kind father-figure. In the reign of Elizabeth the system in general worked well: it had not yet become an excuse for unscrupulous employers to obtain cheap, or even free, labour by exploiting helpless orphans—a device of which the Industrial Revolution was to furnish many horrid examples. The apprentice was still part of the family, and "the average man does not like to see unhappy faces at his own board and in his own household".

Although child labour was of less significance than it became in the 18th century, it already played some part in the cloth industry. Over a hundred years after Elisabeth's time, Daniel Defoe observed that there was hardly a child in the west of England that could not earn its living at the age of five. That was not a new development. The craft of spinning, carried on to a great extent by country women in their homes, had kept very young children employed since the Middle Ages.

On the farms there were many jobs that could be performed by very young children. Bird-scaring was the earliest occupation of the country child, something that he (or she) could do almost as soon as he could toddle. A contemporary account of seasonal duties of the farmer's wife mentions the need to hire children to clear the stones from fallow land. Early 17th-century prints show children assisting their elders in sheepshearing and in capturing a swarm of bees (the child is well wrapped up, with a net over his face). Young children were occupied in loading carts, winnowing the grain, feeding the animals, and many another rustic task.

PRIMARY EDUCATION

Since it was almost exclusively undertaken by religious institutions, education suffered during the Reformation. By about 1600, the disturbance had settled and schools were probably more numerous than before.

Although we know little of primary education in the 16th century, it seems to have been worst affected by the revolution of the 1530s. Before the Reformation, it had been mainly undertaken by chantry priests, who were endowed by the dead to say masses for their souls and usually had plenty of time for other tasks, like teaching. The abolition of chantries by Henry VIII destroyed many of these little schools, but not all. A number managed to keep going with the help of local endowment. Some new schools were started too. Grammar schools occasionally provided primary education where it was not otherwise available. Parish priests, sometimes subsidised, sometimes out of a sense of duty, undertook some instruction of the youngest children.

We should not assume that primary education was ignored simply because it was mainly required by the children of the poorer classes (the children of the gentry being instructed at home). There were probably a great many little establishments of the type that a later age would call "dame schools", where the teacher's qualifications may have been slight, but where the basics of reading and writing were more or less competently taught. A census taken of the poor in Norwich in

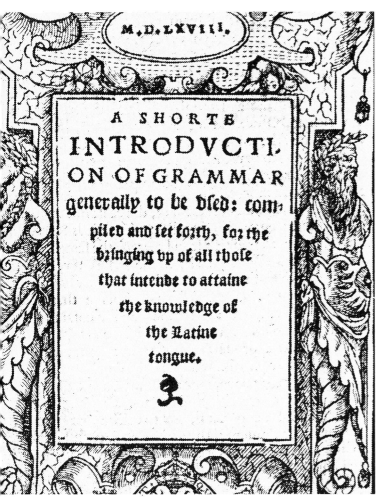

M.D.LXVIII.

A SHORTE
INTRODVCTI
ON OF GRAMMAR
generally to be vsed: compiled and set forth, for the
bringing vp of all those
that intende to attaine
the knowledge of
the Latine
tongue.

1571, which included young children, revealed a considerable number of seven to eight-years-olds attending school. In a village near Leicester there was a chapel at the other end of the village from the parish church which, as it was no longer required for religious services, was turned into a free school. The existence of such schools is discovered now and then by industrious local historians: they do not appear in official records, and we can assume there were many more of them than we have direct knowledge of. More of Elizabeth's subjects could read and write than might be supposed, and it has been plausibly suggested that the standard of literacy in the early seventeenth century was higher than it was in the early 19th century, after the disruption of the Industrial Revolution. Since there was no *system* of education, everything depended, as far as poor children were concerned, on local conditions.

Not only was primary education more widespread than has generally been assumed, it was also less sexually exclusive. Although women were destined for a domestic role in life, it was an advantage for them also to be able to read and write (which was all that primary education taught). We would certainly expect to find fewer girls than boys in a village school room, and in many villages, no doubt, no girls at all. Nevertheless, there are recorded instances of girl pupils, which are not qualified by the suggestion that this was in any way unusual. Only daughters of the rich received a full academic education, and then but rarely. When a scholarly young woman was presented to James I, he said only "Can she spin?"

Children learned to read from a hornbook. This was originally a flat, paddle-shaped piece of wood attached to which was a sheet bearing the letters of the alphabet, with some further combinations of letters and, very often, the Lord's Prayer at the foot. It was covered with a thin sheet of horn—the 16th-century equivalent of PVC—to protect it. The first book that the young Shakespeare and his fellows would have read would probably have been a combined alphabet-book and catechism.

The style of handwriting being taught to children was in the process of change during the late 16th century. The hand Shakespeare used, to judge by the signatures which are the only examples of his handwriting we have, was the old medieval hand. In this respect he was a little old-fashioned, as the new, rounder Italian hand, more like modern handwriting and corresponding to *Italic* in printing, was already established in England.

Many children received their primary education at home, from their mother or some other relation. In the homes of the gentry and nobility there was sometimes a domestic chaplain who would undertake the teaching of the younger children of the household, or even a tutor hired specifically for that job. As these households were frequently large, the tutor might have a sizeable class. If he were notably well qualified, neighbours might send their children, so that a genuine school was created. And this was not necessarily limited to primary education: it might go up to university level.

The custom among the nobility and gentry to send their sons to live in another house, often of a grander kinsman, was a medieval one. It continued in Elizabeth's time. The son and heir of a landed family living in north-west England, or some other relatively rough region, might be sent to a house in the home counties. Edward Herbert of Cherbury was heir to some estates in Wales and was therefore sent to live in a learned Welsh household with the idea that, among other accomplishments, he should learn to speak Welsh. (As it happened, he was a poor linguist and, he regretfully admitted in later years, he made little progress in Welsh or any other language.)

GRAMMAR SCHOOLS

We know more about grammar schools (secondary schools) in Elizabeth's time than we know about primary schools. They also received a severe blow at the Reformation, though perhaps less serious than the effect of the abolition of chantries on primary education. For secondary education also, the blow was less serious than it seemed and its effects were quite rapidly overcome. The old cathedral and monastic schools were re-established as secular institutions. Many of them were soon flourishing more vigorously than they ever had under monastic control. Some schools did disappear, but not a great number and, as a rule, only the smallest. Secular schools, like Eton and Winchester, also suffered at the Reformation because, although not actually religious foundations, they were willy-nilly largely under religious control, virtually all teachers being in holy orders.

There are, or were until recently, a relatively large number of schools in England called "King Edward VI's School". People often assume that Edward, the bookish son of Henry VIII who died in his teens, was a great founder of grammar schools, and this myth is still sometimes encountered in books. But the schools named after Edward VI were (most of them anyway) merely old monastic or cathedral schools under a new, nationalistic name.

However, many new schools were founded in Shakespeare's time, including some famous ones which are still going strong, such as Harrow, Rugby and Shrewsbury. These names now seem quintessentially "ruling-class", but it was not so in the 16th century. Their founders were seldom great aristocrats: the founder of Harrow was a wealthy yeoman, the founder of Dulwich College an actor and impresario. The four still-surviving Welsh schools founded in the reign of Elizabeth owe their existence respectively to a lawyer, a clergyman, a peer and a draper. Some schools were founded by craft guilds, primarily for the sons of their own members. A notable example is Merchant Taylors, possibly the most progressive school in England when Shakespeare's contemporary, Richard Mulcaster, was its headmaster. Mulcaster's view of the purpose of education was startlingly modern: "to help nature to her perfection in the complete development of all the various powers... whereby each shall be best able to perform all those functions in life which his position shall require, whether public or private..." (quoted by A.L. Rowse).

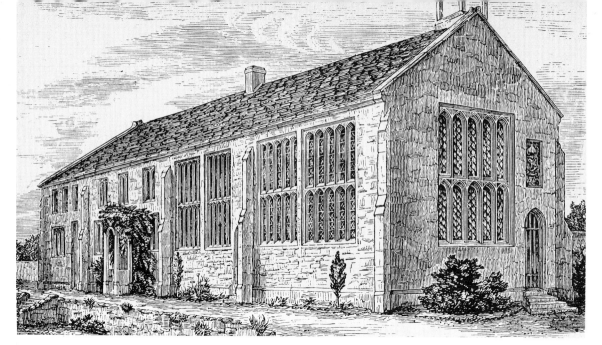

Left, the Grammar School *at Taunton. Above, a library; note that the books are chained.*

One of the most successful schools in Elizabethan England was Shrewsbury, which attracted the sons of many of the gentry from North Wales and north-west England. Some peers' sons also attended, but so did local boys, not all of whom were the sons of the leading citizens. Like a number of other schools, Shrewsbury was to some extent under the control of a university college (St. John's, Cambridge) which shared the responsibility with the town authorities and the headmaster.

The need for education was clearly recognised: there was a well-known saying, "Better to be unborn than untaught". Elizabethan England was fortunate in having several keen, capable and determined educationists who accomplished much more than they could have done with their own talents and purses alone by their skill as fundraisers. One of the most energetic was Alexander Nowell. Dean of St Paul's. Dr. A.L. Rowse has recounted one anecdote of his efforts for education.

A rich widow lost her only son in a riding accident. Dean Nowell visited her in an attempt to reconcile her to the will of God. He was unsuccessful but God, he says, gave him the notion to say to the widow, "Comfort yourself... and I will tell you how you shall have twenty sons to comfort you in these sorrows... who would be in love towards you as dear children". (Quoted Rowse *The England of Elizabeth* 1950, page 499). This desirable result was to be achieved, needless to say, by endowments to education. The widow bequeathed her fortune for the founding of Newport Grammar School and of several scholarships to the universities.

By the end of the 16th century, England possibly had more grammar schools than it had before the Reformation. William Harrison, author of a contemporary *Description of England*, reckoned that nearly every corporate town had a school, though many of these would have had only one schoolmaster (or mistress: most, but not all, teachers were men).

The teaching of these schools, old and new, was still medieval, not to say ancient Roman. According to one contemporary schoolmaster, the reason a boy came to school was to learn to be a good man, in order to give the best service to Prince and country and to help his parents, himself and his family. But it must be said that the usual curriculum seemed but ill designed to meet these requirements. The use of printed books clearly made an enormous difference to education, but in Elizabeth's time it had yet to make more than a superficial impression on the subjects taught or the manner of teaching.

The medieval curriculum was based on the seven "liberal arts" of the *trivium* (grammar, logic and rhetoric) and the *quadrivium* (arithmetic, geometry, astronomy and music). It hardly needs to be said that what was then understood by astronomy would not be so described nowadays. Basically, what this system taught was Latin, and yet more Latin. "Grammar" meant Latin grammar. English literature was not taught at all. It may seem perverse to condemn a system from which emerged a Shakespeare, a Marlowe, a Spenser, and a dozen other fine poets. Nevertheless, the curriculum does not seem attuned to the needs of the average student, and it was, indeed, criticised by the more progressive educationists of the time, such as Roger Ascham (former tutor to the young Elizabeth) and Richard Mulcaster. The latter advocated teaching

English as an academic subject, but his appeal met with small response. (There was of course almost a complete absence of books for such a subject.)

One contemporary writer speaks of a mistress teaching a child to read with alphabet in one hand and a stick in the other. Corporal punishment in the 16th and 17th centuries was frequent and savage. Thomas Tusser, who tells us many interesting details about life in Elizabethan England in his lively and unpretentious verse, remarks how, at Eton in the 1530s, he received no less than 53 stripes. More horrific stories can be found in other sources, though some must be either exaggerated or untypical. But one notable feature of almost every contemporary woodcut showing a schoolroom, and there are many, is a large bundle of birch twigs, resembling something to sweep the floor rather than chastise the lazy, disobedient or, alas, merely slow-witted child. Some school seals show the master beating a pupil, as if this were the school's chief *raison d'être*.

As punishments were no less—perhaps more— ferocious at some schools in the 19th century, we need not be shocked by the violence which was so large a part of 16th and 17th-century education. More surprising is the attitude of educators like Roger Ascham who deplored the harsh discipline and flogging prevalent in most schools. Teachers were no more brutal than parents, of course, and another royal pupil, Lady Jane Grey (she was briefly declared queen on the death of Edward VI in an unsuccessful attempt to bar Catholic Mary Tudor from the throne) remembered her tuition by a kindly scholar, so different from her harsh parents, as the happiest days of her short life.

Roger Ascham thought that children should have games, and that school ought to be a place where they could play; but in this too he was far ahead of his time. Games were regarded much as novel-reading was regarded two centuries later—frivolous, slightly shameful and of no value. Schools therefore offered little in the way of sport. Football was banned, anyway. However, the better schools at least were not entirely without forms of recreation. In particular, and as befitted the greatest age of English drama, play-acting was very popular. Ben Jonson indeed lamented that so many plays were put on by schools that the professional actor was in danger of losing his livelihood. Mulcaster's boys of Merchant Taylors' School performed on several occasions before the Queen. Other London schools, like St Paul's and Westminster, also gave performances of plays.

School hours were extremely long, beginning soon after dawn and continuing (in winter) until dusk. There was a widespread feeling that education should be free, although Mulcaster thought that fees ought to be charged as an incentive. Most schools existed to serve the local population, and they were often sufficiently well endowed that only a small fee, if any at all, had to be charged. Shreswsbury charged only an entrance fee, which was graded according to the social standing of the father: it was only fourpence for the son of a local burgess. Harrow, one of the comparatively few schools which catered to boys from distant parts, admitted without charge forty local boys, who might be either rich or poor. At Stratford Grammar School, the young William Shakespeare cost his father nothing, except what it cost to buy his satchel, books, pens, ink, etc.

Above, the entrance to a college at Cambridge, and, right, Oxford as it was in Elizabethan times.

OXFORD AND CAMBRIDGE

The curriculum at universities differed little from that in the schools, although there was somewhat more evidence of the Renaissance "New Learning". Even so, the kind of astronomy being taught at Oxford during the reign of Elizabeth owed nothing whatever to Copernicus. Those who wanted a "modern" education would have been better advised to get it from books (they would have learned far more about geography, for instance, from the pages of Richard Hakluyt, the historian of 16th-century voyages, than they would from Latin orations and disputations), although there were institutions with a more modern outlook, notably Gresham's College in London, where the forerunners of the men who founded the Royal Society (1662) received intellectual nourishment.

Oxford and Cambridge, particularly the former, suffered seriously at the Reformation because, unlike many schools, they could scarcely hope to escape the attention of the reformers. Purges and counter-purges wreaked havoc not only with personnel but also materials: books that gave the slightest offence to the prevailing ideology were

burnt. The universities were, and remained, peculiarly sensitive to political changes (someone referred to them as the two eyes of the state). The government kept in close touch with university matters, and it is no coincidence that the chancellors of Oxford and Cambridge in the reign of Elizabeth were respectively Leicester, the Queen's favourite subject, and Burghley, her most intimate counsellor.

"Universities do wondrously decay", said Bishop Latimer about 1550, but fifty years later the situation was transformed: in the reign of Elizabeth both Oxford and Cambridge recovered and progressed. One sign was the foundation of new colleges—two at Cambridge, one at Oxford. Like the schools, the universities benefitted from the fashion for educational endowment. These were no doubt most useful in cash, but endowments of a different sort were hardly less valuable. The Earl of Essex, for example, gave to Thomas Bodley, founder of the Bodleian Library at Oxford, a valuable Spanish library which had come into his possession through the fortunes of war.

Although the curriculum changed little, the system of education was undergoing considerable alteration, the most important aspects of which

were the greater significance of colleges and the growth of the tutorial system. Before the Reformation, the colleges had been for the most part small and cramped, providing residence for a few graduates only; undergraduates lived in lodgings or inns. In Shakespeare's day the colleges insisted on residence, and they provided teaching themselves, as well as the lectures provided by the university.

Students often lived in the same room as their tutor, who thus had close control over their activities. Occasionally, students brought their own tutor from home, though colleges were not eager to bestow fellowships on tutors who were graduates of other institutions. Although the new system was less democratic, possibly less fun, than the old system, in which discipline had been maintained, so far as it was maintained at all, by older students, the universities became more orderly, and parents were no longer quite so reluctant to send their sons to these former dens of disorder. However, there was no call for complacency.

A university education was not expensive. A very good room at one Oxford college could be rented for £1 a year, and an adequate one for half that. Meals for a month in the college hall, where there were three tables at which the diners (and the quality of the food) were segregated by social status, cost about £1. Poor students could economise in various ways. Sharing rooms was a common expedient, and some earned a few pence by acting as servants to richer students, rather in the way that at English boarding schools until quite recently younger boys performed odd jobs for older boys. Though vacations were shorter than today (only 12 days at Christmas and Easter), poor students at Cambridge took temporary jobs working on the roads around the town, or in the fields at harvest, or at Stourbridge fair.

There is a well-known passage by William Harrison which complains that the universities are full of rich men's sons and are becoming places of idleness and extravagance. Most modern historians are doubtful of these strictures. Certainly there were more sons of the nobility and gentry at the

universities. In spite of the discontent of Burghley's grandson, writing to him from St. John's, Cambridge, that "I could be very well content to go from hence as soon as might be", the nobility no longer regarded learning as beneath their dignity, and the universities no longer catered almost exclusively to aspiring clergymen. Out of 100 undergraduates at one Cambridge college in 1564, there was one nobleman's son, 13 from the ranks of the upper gentry, seventeen from the lower gentry, 59 who may be called (in slightly anachronistic shorthand) "middle-class", and 10 poor men's sons.

As for the extravagance of the idle rich, the rules against all forms of behaviour that might be so classed, from frequenting taverns or going hawking or even growing the hair too long, were numerous and strict. That of course may be interpreted as a sign that the activities regulated against did exist on a large scale (otherwise the rules would have been unnecessary), but on the whole it seems that the students of Elizabethan England were not notably more disorderly than modern students. Nor is there much evidence of aristocratic extravagance. The Earl of Essex, when an undergraduate, had his windows glazed and spent about £1 on a table and other furnishings for his room: hardly the height of extravagance.

The arts degree course, leading to an M.A., took seven years (the same time as a craft apprenticeship) but at Cambridge it was already the custom to do a "bachelor's" course, for four years, returning after another three to deliver the disputation that earned an M.A. The hours of work were probably less demanding than at school, as there was less constant supervision. But life could be hard for the "poor, godly, diligent students" of St. John's, Cambridge, who rose before five, attended chapel between five and six, studied till ten and dined on "a penny piece of beef among four", studied again until an equally spartan supper at five and then again until nine or ten, when they went to bed, after half an hour's vigorous exercise to warm themselves up, since they could not afford a fire.

Undergraduates were much younger than now, many boys going up to university at thirteen. It is thus less incongruous than it at first seems to learn that university students were flogged as frequently as schoolboys.

The total population of both universities was estimated in Elizabeth's reign as 3,000, a larger

number, certainly, than ever before. Cambridge, the junior establishment until the Reformation, had caught up with Oxford in numbers and in general reputation was pulling ahead. Queen Elizabeth was associated more with Cambridge, most of her ministers and bishops, like her tutors as a girl, being Cambridge men. Cambridge also seems to have been intellectually the more vigorous. This was without doubt largely due to the stimulus, often a far from comfortable one, of Puritanism. Well represented at both universities, Puritanism was stronger at Cambridge, situated in what is traditionally a strongly Puritan region (East Anglia). One professor of divinity was removed from his chair for advocating a presbyterian church, but Burghley as chancellor, being sympathetic to the Puritans but committed to peace and the stability of the Elizabethan Church settlement, smoothed over most potential conflicts. Cambridge also suffered less than the older and larger university from the departure of Roman Catholics after 1570, when most English Catholics went to continental universities. In other respects too, Cambridge seemed more progressive: among all the rules and regulations, the students were at least permitted to play football.

5. HOUSE AND HOME

THE COUNTRY HOUSE

The prosperous, vigorous gentry who inevitably dominate the history of England in the late 16th and early 17th centuries were responsible for the first great age of the country house, that most distinctively English contribution to European architecture. Apart from those built from scratch, there was hardly a house of any significance which was not altered and enlarged in this period. The strong central government which England had since the end of the Wars of the Roses had won the conflict (at least in most of the country) with those powerful subjects who had ruled their regions like petty princes secure in stone-walled castles. Gunpowder and the Tudors put an end to private fortresses, and peace made them unnecessary. The last castles were built in the reign of Henry VIII, and they were built by the royal government, to defend important harbours.

Before the Reformation, an excess of wealth was often devoted to the Church. The finest parish churches in England are to be found in East Anglia and the West Country, the two leading wool-growing, and therefore richest, regions of late medieval England. There was little church-building in the 16th century. Where once men had built churches to the glory of the Virgin Mother, they now built great houses to entertain the Virgin Queen. (But if the Queen really slept in as many different places as local legends insist, she must have seldom spent two nights in the same place).

The Elizabethans, said Sir John Neale, "indulged in pleasures as if they were to die tomorrow, and built as if they were to live for ever". The great houses of Elizabethan England exemplify many of the virtues and many of the vices of society—energy, optimism, sheer high spirits on the one hand; rampant materialism and the desire to show off on the other. Absorbing continental influences

The traditional English country house achieved its finest style in Elizabethan times (photo on left). Below, the famous Longleat Castle.

As soon as the fine weather came, at least part of the day was spent in the garden, as shown in the prints of two Lancashire manor houses (opposite).

like a thirsty sponge, their builders flung together styles drawn often uncomprehendingly from—chiefly—Italy, and from France, Flanders and elsewhere together with the traditional English Gothic: the result was sometimes indisputably vulgar; but time is a great refiner, and even a house like Kirby Hall in Northamptonshire, which amazingly combines classical Greece with the English Middle Ages and the Italian Renaissance, seems appealing now. Eclecticism also made for variety: scarcely two great Elizabethan houses look alike.

Some of the most remarkable buildings of the time have long disappeared, including Burghley's great house of Theobald's, where the Queen, unimpressed by the five courtyards, complained of the smallness of her bedchamber, compelling immediate reconstruction. (The enormous 17th-century mansion of his immediate descendants, Hatfield, still stands and is one of the most popular tourist attractions in England.) Gone too is the Queen's favourite palace. Nonsuch, the gilded exterior of which, in a setting sun, made it look from a distance as though it were on fire. But others, hardly less grand, remain.

One of the first great houses of the reign of Elizabeth, Longleat, is still inhabited by the descendants of its first owner, Sir John Thynne. His master builder was Robert Smythson, who also built Wollaton Hall, with its spectacular towers and lofty hall, in Nottinghamshire. Another house designed by Smythson, Hardwick Hall, with its great expanses of window, is the greatest memorial of a memorable woman, Bess of Hardwick, who survived four husbands in succession and devoted the fortunes of each to building houses. It is strictly anachronistic to call Smythson an "architect", although the man usually described as the first architect in England, and the first to truly comprehend the rules of the classical orders of architecture, Inigo Jones (1573-1652), was his near-contemporary.

Yet these ostentatious palaces were not typical. Their builders ignored Francis Bacon's dictum: houses are built to be lived in, not to be looked on. Nor were they typically English, as the English architectural tradition is essentially unostentatious. Much closer to the tradition is a house like Mapledurham, near Reading, and the large but unpretentious manor houses still widely scattered over the face of England, many of which are reconstructed or expanded medieval buildings.

As Bacon warned, the first necessity in building a house was to choose a good site. There had to be gardens, orchards, a park, with wood, water and other requisites easily available. Surviving houses are evidence of their builders' eye for a good site, although there was a curious fashion among the wealthy to build their houses facing north, the southern prospect being thought unhealthy.

To compensate for chilly north winds, there was often a room built especially to catch the sun, while houses generally were better heated. Coal was extensively mined in the 16th century, and many a country gentleman burned coal from his own estate in his own fireplace. Needless to say, the greatly increased construction of fireplaces was regarded by some contemporaries as degenerate, and responsible for an alleged vulnerability to coughs and colds: one heard exactly the same criticism of central heating a few years ago. The great fireplace with its decoratively carved mantel was a new and characteristic feature. So was its concomitant chimney, a rarity before 1500, the novelty of which encouraged Turor builders to make them an extravagantly decorative, if sometimes ill-matched, feature of the house.

The old medieval courtyard was disappearing, except in really vast palaces, in favour of E and H-shaped houses. The medieval hall was being replaced by separate dining and drawing rooms, while the cooking, which had once taken place at the central fire, was relegated to a separate kitchen. Glass replaced horn or wooden shutters in the windows which, no longer restricted by military considerations, were large and well-proportioned. The new lightness which large windows permitted indoors was heightened by the use of plaster for ceilings, sometimes in highly decorative, abstract designs.

The larger houses usually contained that attractive feature, the long gallery (in some cases 60 m long), which came to be a picture gallery though in Elizabethan times it was more often hung with tapestries or panelled. It was used for games of bowls, sword practice and other forms of exercise.

The long gallery was reached by a wide and elegant stairway, ornately carved. Strange as it seems, England was already experiencing the beginnings of a timber shortage—enough to make wooden houses rare in the south-east, although there was more use of wood inside, with oak (often

imported) wainscoting becoming popular. Oak, according to one contemporary (Harrison), had previously been restricted to churches and religious houses, noblemen's lodgings and shipbuilding, but was now found everywhere. Except in a few areas boarded houses were still erected, timber was mostly seen structurally in the familiar form of black-and-white half-timbering.

LESSER HOUSES

It was not only the gentry and aristocracy who were great builders in the late 16th century. Yeomen, on their more modest scale (though some yeoman were indistinguishable from some gentry), were no less enterprising, and there was as much construction of small farms and cottages as there was of grander houses. Unlike their richer fellow-subjects, they were less concerned with questions of contemporary fashion and knew little or nothing of architectural developments. They could not be bothered with such fads as the avoidance of a supposedly debilitating southern prospect and they could not afford to import fancy building materials, still less foreign craftsmen like those who worked on many of the great Elizabethan houses.

Their buildings were therefore closer to the country, to the soil from which they grew. They used the most easily available materials: stone houses were built only in regions where there were good stone quarries as, for example, in the west of England and parts of the east midlands. Where there was no stone they used brick, or most famously in north-west England, near the Welsh border, half-timbered plaster. Their plaster was of very good quality, often mixed with cow-dung and straw. Roofs were frequently thatched, which is cosy but apt to catch fire. It was washed with lime to prevent it catching light from sparks, and the profusion of new chimneys (singled out by one contemporary witness as a marked feature of the changes he had witnessed, much as we, looking at the same houses, might remark on the recent accession of television aerials) reduced the danger of setting fire to the thatch, though the sheer number of fires where none had existed before probably ensured that there were more, rather than fewer, houses burned down.

As in larger houses, fireplaces were capacious. The main supporting beam of the chimneypiece

was sometimes carved with the owner's initials. Farmhouse fireplaces sometimes had that intriguing feature, an inglenook—a corner inside the fireplace where a seat could be placed, or hams hung to be cured in the warm and smoky atmosphere. Glazed windows were becoming common even in quite modest houses, and the floors were stone slabs, without foundations. Humbler cottages still had earth floors.

Ordinary houses were narrow, with steeply pitched roofs, which often formed the walls of the upper floor. Downstairs there was perhaps only one room, with a central fireplace, though more usually it was divided into two or three. The master bedroom occupied a central position on the upper floor with male children and servants on one side and females on the other. Everyone had to pass through the master bedroom on the way to his or her quarters. There were no passages or corridors, as a rule, in houses of this size, and if there was a third floor, in the loft, access to it was often by a separate, outside staircase. As so much food had to be stored for winter, a loft and a cellar were desirable, and there were also various outhouses.

Town houses were generally similar to corresponding houses in the country except that, space being restricted, they were usually smaller. Nevertheless, there was room for very large houses even within the City of London's walls—witness the mansion of the great financier, Sir Thomas Gresham,

Left, Elizabethan house, and, below, the familiar interior of Dr. John Hall, Stratford.

founder of the Royal Exchange. Others preferred to build outside the city walls. London merchants lived in houses not dissimilar in shape from the London houses of today—tall, with several storeys, and narrow, with long gardens at the rear. Each storey overhung the one below, so the best rooms were at the top of the house. Curiously, those who could afford something larger tended to build their town house to look like two or three ordinarily sized houses side by side.

Very little survives of London as it was in Elizabeth's time, much having perished in the fire of 1666. (A well-known block of half-timbered houses in Holborn, though genuinely Elizabethan in origin, has been much altered in the course of time.) But there are many examples of whole streets and districts in provincial towns and cities, like Elm Hill in Norwich which still look today as they did nearly 400 years ago.

Of the houses (if that is the right word for what was usually a one-room shed) of the very poor, practically nothing remains. Indeed, from Saxon times up to the 19th century, there is remarkably little evidence of the poorest houses, tiny homes of turf, or triangular wooden sheds without floor, chimney, windows or even "walls". The commonest form of building at this level was mud on a rough timber frame. The mud was mixed with straw and laid on in layers. Similar methods were used in parts of the south-west for more substantial houses and, protected by an overhanging thatched roof, they proved surprisingly durable.

SANITATION

However superficially attractive they may be, the English houses of three or four hundred years ago were inevitably dirty, smelly and unhealthy. The practice of strewing rushes on the floor was still common in Elizabeth's day, in spite of the painfully vivid criticisms of Erasmus of this practice (in fact Erasmus probably exaggerated the nastiness of the system: the rushes were changed more often than he suggested). Carpets were still mainly for hanging or for table covers, although they were beginning to be used in the modern way. Otherwise, floors were covered with matting, or left bare.

Hygiene was not a strong point. For the reason why the death rate was higher in the towns than in the country, it was only necessary to look at the piles of filth that, despite bye-laws, accumulated in streets. Now and then, especially when epidemics were raging, the town government would make extra efforts to enforce the by-laws against dumping dirt in the streets or the rivers and streams that were the only sewers, but the effort was always short-lived. In 1588, the Fleet River, London's main watercourse apart from the Thames herself, was cleaned out, but by James I's reign it was as choked-up and foul-smelling as before. The district of Houndsditch in London is said to derive its name from the dead "hounds" that were flung into the "ditch" running nearby. Yet in some ways, London was better off than other towns. Early in the 17th century a "new river" was dug which gave a supply of fresh water, and even in the 16th century London had a rudimentary water system, mainly for fire-fighting, which was carried in lead pipes. Medieval castles sometimes had compartments, often sociably twin-seated, with an open drain into the moat, or into a channel dug to connect with a nearby stream, but the Elizabethan house often depended on buckets or chamber pots, which were emptied by hand on the nearest (often too near) dung heap. In large houses, however, there was a separate latrine chamber.

In the 1590s, while Shakespeare was writing his history plays and early comedies, Sir John Harington, a man born with greater social advantages (the Queen was his godmother), was exercising his own creative imagination. He invented the water-closet. It seems to have been in principle almost identical with the modern article, consisting of a stone pedestal, a cistern, with pipes and a brass sluice. In the diagram that Harington published of his invention, each part was carefully costed and ornamental fish were shown disporting themselves in the tank. He publicised it in a work called *The Metamorphosis of Ajax*, a rather laboured classical pun (an old word for privy being "jax" or "jakes") which was typical of Harington, one of those witty men who very soon become boring.

The Queen was sufficiently impressed with the new convenience to have one installed in her palace at Richmond, but not many of her subjects followed her example. The water closet was still a rarity in English houses in the 18th century.

FURNITURE

The most important room in the house for people in Elizabethan England was the bedroom. There, the most important happenings of their life took place. There they were conceived; there they were born; there they begot children in their turn; there they gave birth; and there, eventually, they died. Anyone who has inspected collections of 16th century wills, so fruitful a source of information about the lives of ordinary people, cannot doubt that the most important article of furniture in an ordinary household was the bed. (One of the most famous bequests in history is that of Shakespeare to his wife of his "second-best bed"—an enigmatic provision which has prompted much speculation on their relationship.)

Even in humble cottages, wooden pillows had vanished except in spartan homes and feather mattresses had appeared, although the actual bed was simple. The four-posted bed, with canopy, was the pride of larger houses; indeed, if there was only one piece of furniture in the house with any pretension to grandeur, it was the bed. All else might be plain and rustic, while the bed might have a carved and arcaded headboard, elaborately turned posts and tester (no longer a separate item suspended from the ceiling). The whole thing was immensely weighty and often exceedingly large, though the Great Bed of Ware (mentioned by Shakespeare and now in the Victoria and Albert Museum), which could sleep a dozen in fair comfort, must have always been a bit of a freak.

Beds had no springs, but a network of rope on which was laid a straw pallet. Feather mattresses were placed on top. Sheets were of linen, and to

climb between them when fresh from the lavender-scented press must have been an experience as pleasant as it was rare. Woollen blankets were laid on top, with an embroidered coverlet over all.

Life was becoming much more comfortable for most people, and this fact was reflected in the furniture. For one thing, there was more of it. Chairs, which had once been ceremonial thrones reserved for bishops in cathedrals and a few other exalted personages, were now familiar objects, although courtiers still sat on stools while the Queen was more comfortably seated in a chair. Stools and settles were still common—and virtually the only furniture in humble homes—but leather-covered and even upholstered chairs were made by the end of the 16th century, and there are literary references to day-beds, the forerunners of the settee and the chaise longue. Early chairs were usually squareish, with panelled backs, but various different types becoming popular by the end of the century, including X-shaped chairs, with gilt decoration and cushions. Just as joint stools were used as tables as often as seats, chairs often incorporated other functions. Some had a chest below the seat, others could be converted into a table by lowering the back.

In the Middle Ages, the chief container for storage was the chest, but by Elizabeth's time someone had thought of adding a pair of drawers to the chest, the first step towards producing a "chest of drawers". The cupboard took on new forms in the press and the wardrobe, and a characteristic piece was the "court cupboard", or buffet, a cross between cupboard and sideboard, for displaying the family plate. Tables generated several new types, including various expandable forms, among them the ancestor of the ever-popular "gate-leg" table. Dining tables, rectangular in shape, betrayed their origin as trestle tables. They had heavy stretchers at floor level.

If this was the first great age of English furniture, it cannot be regarded as aesthetically satisfying. In general, it suffered from the same faults as the more grandiose buildings—flamboyance without subtlety, a wish to show off combined with a careless amalgam of ill-digested foreign influences.

Above, the furniture of the room in which Shakespeare was born. Right, table, bench and stools from the Elizabethan period. Four-poster canopy beds came into fashion (print and photo, bottom left and right).

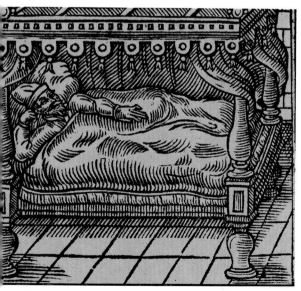

All furniture was of oak: it tended to be massive, and very heavily carved. These characteristics grew more pronounced towards the end of the period. Classical decorative motifs—acanthus leaves, Greek fretwork, swags and pilasters—covered indiscriminately any vacant space, and a characteristic innovation was what is called "melon bulb" turning—a great, swelling, vase-like form on turned members such as table legs. (In spite of its weight, the Queen took her own furniture with her on her summer travels: 400 carts were required.)

The best furniture was sometimes inlaid with a chequered pattern in holly or boxwood, as in the "Nonsuch" chests, so-called because they bore an inlaid representation of the palace of that name. These chests may have originated outside England, perhaps in Germany, being copied later by English craftsmen.

The style of the Elizabethan period was highly ornamental—perhaps excessively so, as can be seen from this wash-basin and clock (opposite).

HOUSEHOLD ARTICLES

The ornate display cupboards that increasingly took their place in the long galleries of great houses were designed to show off the family collection of plate. Silver had become plentiful in Europe through the exploitation of Spanish American mines, and a fair proportion of it found its way, somehow or other, into England. Formerly, silver had been restricted to the houses of noblemen, but in Elizabethan times you could see a fine collection in the houses of gentlemen and merchants of average wealth. Quite humble households would possess at least a silver salt, an object which still possessed its ancient ritualistic significance. As there were no banks, silver was a good investment, the best after land—and more easily negotiable.

Silver replaced pewter vessels, just as pewter, which was not cheap, replaced the still humbler wooden platters and leather jugs of earlier times. Knives were already made in the traditional centre of the English cutlery industry, Sheffield, and spoons were favoured as christening presents. They were made in fanciful designs, including the popular "apostle" handles. Forks made their first appearance in Elizabeth's reign, but it is doutbtful if they were in general use. The Queen had several gold ones, given as presents at different times.

Ornamental cups and tankards were also useful as presents. The Queen had some gold ones, but besides gold, silver-gilt and silver, they were sometimes made out of other materials, such as alabaster, ivory or glass. Ewers and bowls, much in use at a time when food was handled without a fork, were also made of silver, and occasionally crystal. Other articles in silver found in wealthy households were spice and perfume boxes, often set with precious stones, Nuremberg nefs containing napkins, condiments, etc, pomanders and pouncet boxes, andirons and candlesticks. Whether free-standing or mounted, candleholders had previously been of brass or iron or occasionally, in poorer houses, of wood. By the 17th century elaborate chandeliers were in use although there are no survivals from earlier than the Civil War (1642-45), during which so much English plate was melted down. Decent candlesticks were reserved for good candles; candles made of Russian tallow, which burnt unevenly, spattered fat about and smelt horrible, were not put in silver candlesticks.

"As for glassmakers, they be scant in the land" wrote a poet in 1557, though he went on to praise the skill of a glassmaker who worked in Sussex. There were sufficient glassmakers in that area thirty years later for the government to shut them down because it considered them a threat to the iron and shipbuilding industries, with which they competed for fuel, i.e. timber. However, the days when English glass would challenge the best in Europe lay in the future, and the best glass was "Venice glass". There were one or two Venetian glassmakers in London in the mid 16th century, but most of the fragments that survive from the 16th century are of green, thick glass. It is clear that glass was commonly used for drinking vessels; Shakespeare's Falstaff regarded them as most suitable for that activity. And there, indisputably, spoke an expert.

Pottery was not much in favour. German stoneware jugs, sometimes silver-mounted, were in use for ale, and some types of red ware were fairly common. The so-called "green ware" with relief decoration which was made in the 16th century disappeared in the early 17th century. But there were potteries turning out slipware and earthenware with a hard, brown, lead glaze. A characteristic vessel was the tyg, a cup with several handles, which was probably passed from hand to hand. All English pottery was stout rustic stuff, not to be found in elegant households.

GARDENS AND ORCHARDS

The English, everyone knows, love gardens. They have done so since Elizabeth's time, indeed earlier no doubt, though William Harrison, writing in the 1580s, said the popular interest in gardening was a phenomenon of the previous forty years. Every house had (and has) its garden, in the town no less than the country. Hatton Garden, now the centre of London's jewellery trade, was once the garden of Sir Christopher Hatton, Queen Elizabeth's vice-chancellor. Covent Garden had a similar origin. The garden was almost as important as the house and was equally a sign of the prosperity of its owner. At Theobald's, Lord Burghley's house in Hertfordshire, there were four gardens including the kitchen garden, and about forty poor people were employed there weekly as casual labour, apart from the regular gardeners. Gardens were also a sign of the relative security of the times. One does not lay out flowerbeds and plant shrubs unless one can feel reasonably certain they will be able to grow in peace, and not be ridden over by troops or bandits.

The layout of a garden in the 16th century was entirely different from a modern English garden, with its gentle landscaping and general proximity to nature. The gardens of Shakespeare's time were more formal, laid out in geometric patterns like the patterns on furniture, and rather resembling the design of certain oriental carpets (the art had come from the East with the Crusaders). The simplest design, recommended by Bacon in his essay *Of Gardens,* was a square, divided into four smaller squares with some centrepiece such as a fountain or small pavilion.

For gardens were not all flowers. From the house, one would emerge on to a terrace, with low balustrade. There might be further terraces and a variety of other striking features. There was a fountain at Kenilworth, the Earl of Leicester's home, elaborately carved from marble, with figures of marine creatures such as sea horses and dolphins, together with Tritons and Nereids: fish swam in the basins and the spray was so powerful that the spectator had to keep his distance or risk a soaking. In other gardens, he might get soaked deliberately by a joke spray and there was a sundial at one place which, as the visitor bent to examine it, released a fountain into his face. The Elizabethans were not averse to rather rough practical jokes.

A large garden was likely also to contain stone sculptures and fish ponds, though Bacon refused to recommend ponds on the grounds that they attracted frogs and flies. Nor was he keen on the fashion for having some beds free of flowers but containing a design in varicoloured sands. There were summer houses with, if possible, one on a raised mount with a view over the countryside, and there were even banquet houses, like the one at Hampton Court, far removed from the house and the kitchens, and surely serving cold food. As in the large house, nothing was too exotic if it made a good show. Sir Walter Raleigh diverted a river to flow through his rockery; Lord Cobham had an arbour on three floors built into a lime tree. The Queen's garden at Whitehall had a large number of standing figures in wood, painted and gilded. But for all this ostentation, Elizabeth's favourite flower was the simple violet, and the most cherished flower in the country at large was the rose.

Flower beds were often symmetrically arranged in "knots" (i.e. "designs"), usually with shrubs forming the outline and flowers planted in between. Such a garden can still be seen at New Place, Stratford-on-Avon, complete with the surrounding high hedges (they should be 3 metres high, according to Bacon).

Topiary was much in fashion, with yew and juniper being skilfully carved into all kinds of shapes, most often birds or animals. Mazes were also popular: one 16th-century example survives at Hampton Court.

The flowers and shrubs grown in a garden over 300 years ago would mostly be familiar today, although we have many flowers that Elizabeth's subjects did not know. Many new flowers were introduced—perhaps as many as 200— in the late 16th and early 17th centuries, and others were being improved. Certain annuals, for example, were turned into perennials. Altogether, there was sufficient innovation to provoke a conservative reaction: the old English flowers were best, said some; away with "outlandish" new ones.

6. FASHION

THE ELIZABETHAN GENTLEMAN

The history of clothes is too often recounted as the history of fashion, something altogether different. However, it is the rich and glamorous who at least reveal the aspirations of humbler folk, in dress as in other customs, so perhaps the Elizabethan dandy is worth attention as something more than a curiosity.

The aim of fashion was to achieve a full, rounded and unbroken line, but a line which bore little relationship to the human figure. As a result, there was much use of whalebone and padding. The general shape aimed at was an hourglass on stalks—wide at the shoulders and hips, narrow in the waist. The great, baggy trunks descending to the knee seem particularly ungainly to the modern eye.

Clothes, like architecture, were on the one hand extravagant and expensive and, on the other, derived from a multitude of foreign sources. The extravagance and eclecticism of the Englishman's dress were notorious on the Continent.

To begin at the beginning: people in the 16th and 17th centuries were not much concerned with underwear, and undoubtedly most of the population wore none at all. Those who did wore only an undershirt or shift. The next garment, for men, was a kind of shorts, or upper stockings, the legs of which might be seen below the trunks; they were held up by string ties. Stockings were gartered at the knee, and by 1600 shoes had, for the first time, raised heels, often made of cork. The two main items, corresponding roughly to the modern trousers and jacket, were the trunks, or breeches, and doublet. The latter was cut with a low waist ending in a point in front and given a prominent convex curve with the aid of padding. A brief "skirt" below the waist concealed the laces attaching it to the trunks. Some doublets were so stiff that the wearer could barely bend at the waist. The doublet often had "wings" at the shoulder, or had sleeves puffed-up in "leg-of-mutton" fashion.

The curious low, pointed waist to the doublet and the short, flaring trunks (sometimes breeches descending to the knee in the Venetian style), were the outstanding characteristics of men's dress when Shakespeare was a young man. There was one other characteristic article, which was to last well into the 17th century, the ruff. This was an extremely elaborate collar of fine lawn or cambric and lace, stiffened with bone, ivory, wood, or steel wire. At the height of the fashion, ruffs were nearly one metre in diameter, making the wearer look like John the Baptist's head on a plate, as someone remarked. In the reign of James I, the falling ruff came into fashion—equally wide but lying flat over shoulders and chest. Portraits of Shakespeare show him wearing a falling ruff.

Sometimes a jerkin was worn over the doublet: it was similarly cut, but looser and unpadded, and it often had loose half-sleeves. Short cloaks or capes, with upstanding collar, sometimes embroidered with gold lace, were common, but clearly more ornamental than functional. Fur-lined cloaks reaching the ground were more useful. Serious or older men, like Lord Burghley, wore a long black gown, with half sleeves.

The court gallant, as seen in famous portraits like those of Raleigh or the (alleged) Earl of Essex by

The extreme sophistication of personal appearance was particularly noticeable in the cuffs worn by both men and women, and also in their footwear, which was sometimes extraordinarily ornate.

Hilliard, did not wear clothes basically different from those of any gentleman of appropriate rank, except that they were more gorgeous and colourful—oranges and reds were popular—and slightly exaggerated—the ruff a little wider, and so forth. He might be cross-gartered in yellow, an eccentricity that Malvolio was talked into in *Twelfth Night*.

But it was not only the courtier who wanted expensive clothes. "The ploughman", wrote Thomas Lodge, "must nowadays have his doublet of the fashion with wide cuts, his garters of fine silk from Granada..." (quoted J.B. Black *The Reign of Elizabeth* O.U.P. 2nd ed 1959, p.268). It was another sign of the prosperity of the age.

There were rules of society which dictated that a man ought to wear clothes according to his station, though they were probably more honoured in the breach than the observance. An apprentice who dressed up in a fine ruff and silk hat for Christmas was fined by the justices, and town authorities made sure that merchants should not dress like courtiers. Anyway, few could afford to dress according to the latest and highest fashion. A pair of ornamental breeches could cost as much as £100, which is a great deal more than one would pay today regardless of the vast decline of the real value of money since the 16th century.

Fashions changed as now, though less rapidly. By the time of Elizabeth's death, plain clothes were becoming more common among the gentry, owing to Puritan influence. The short trunks went out of fashion along with the protruding doublet; boots of soft leather became popular.

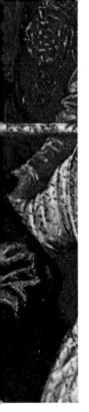

Gentlemen's attire was at least as refined as that of the ladies: brightly coloured fabrics, patterns, all kinds of ornaments, necklaces, chains, emblazoned hose, etc.

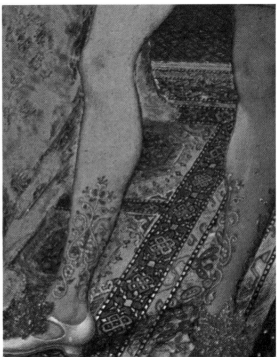

Left, Queen Elizabeth knighting the famous voyager Drake. Bottom, detail of a sword and a symbolic suit of armour made from a medieval design.

WEAPONS AND ARMOUR

A gentleman wore a girdle or belt, which might be silver but was more often leather, from which hung his sword, on a hanger (the word later came to mean the actual sword, often a highly decorative piece itself). Every man carried a weapon—sometimes a rapier and a dagger, sometimes a broadsword, in the case of a poor man probably just a knife. You seldom saw a countryman over 18 or 20 who did not carry a dagger, wrote Harrison. Unfortunately, these weapons were used all too often. Men were quarrelsome, and the swift brandishing of deadly blades in the street was one Italian custom that would have been better *not* imported. Government restrictions did not attempt to ban weapons, but did limit their length, for there was a tendency for swords to grow ever longer. There are occasional references in Shakespeare and elsewhere to a "long sword". This was probably a double-handed weapon.

The rapier was a comparatively new weapon in Elizabethan times, replacing the older type of straight double-edged sword, at least at the side of gentlemen of some pretentions. The earliest rapiers had a cutting edge as well as a thrusting point. Like all novelties, they attracted many opponents, who also deplored the style of fighting with rapier in one hand and dagger in the other. Philip Stubbes, in his attack on the "abuses" of his time, criticised the elaborate hilts and scabbards of contemporary weapons.

Such was the vanity of the Elizabethan knight or gentleman that even his armour, besides being chased, was sometimes garnished with tassels, and his helmet adorned with plumes. His armour was so made that his frilly cuffs and ruff extended beyond it. This was expensive dress armour, specially made, usually in Germany, and very different from the armour supplied to soldiers in the 1580s, which caused many complaints of poor manufacture.

Armour, however, was going slowly out of fashion. Light "half-armour"—a helmet and cuirass —was still usefull in close fighting, but the developing capacities of guns were slowly making armour plate redundant.

Gentlemen often had suits of armour made for themselves (facing, suit belonging to Sir Christopher Hatton).

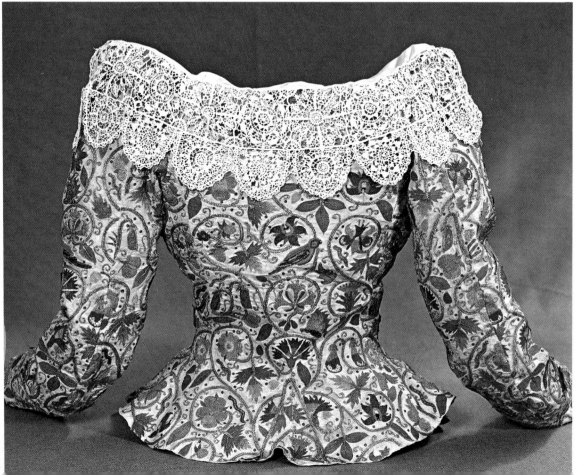

WOMEN'S CLOTHES

Women's clothes, at court and in high society, were hardly less extravagant than men's, and shared many of their characteristics. Ruffs, for example, were worn by both sexes. Blue or yellow starch was sometimes used but plain white was the commoner colour. They were sometimes worn in layers of two or three. The general outline of the figure too was similar to that striven for by men's tailors—wide at the shoulders, tightly corseted at the waist—and wide again at the hips. The width at the shoulder was achieved by padded or puffed-up sleeves. They were detachable and could be regarded as a separate article of clothing, like gloves. They were not necessarily matching: to judge by the popularity of the song. green sleeves were admired.

Rings were very much in fashion... Below, the hands of a gentleman.

The flare at the hips in women's dress was hugely exaggerated by the device called a farthingale—a canvas petticoat on a frame. There were several types. In one, the woman wore a belt over her shift from which projected a kind of rack to support petticoat and skirts: the effect was rather like a cartwheel, with the wearer's waist as the hub. Although the most striking (and, one imagines, least comfortable) effects were attained by this means, some women wore a padded roll around their waists (wider at back and sides than front). This was called the "French" farthingale, to distinguish it from the "Spanish" farthingale.

The bodice was similar to a man's doublet, fairly close-fitting and fastened at one side with hooks; the buttons often appearing down the front were false. It was the custom for girls and unmarried women to expose the upper part of the bosom, and the Queen sometimes wore such dresses. With them it was awkward to wear a ruff, and an alternative was a high upstanding lace collar, held in position by wires, as seen in later portraits of Elizabeth. (There is at least one portrait of the Queen which shows her wearing an ordinary ruff with an exposed bosom, but that particular dress is gathered in again at the throat, leaving a triangle of bare flesh.)

Sometimes, a loose gown was worn over the dress, and hoods could be seen in country districts. Silk stockings were coming into fashion, and shoes, of silk or velvet as well as leather, were raised with cork heels. They were often embroidered.

The dress of the time is best known from portraits of the Queen herself, which naturally represent the highest peak of couture. How she managed to move at all with those enormous sleeves, constricted waist and vast skirts is a puzzle. And surely ladies did not ride a horse in a farthingale? But these dresses were very expensive creations, for ceremonial wear. They were exquisitely embroidered all over, and sometimes studded with jewels. The Queen is said to have possessed 300 of them when she died, but they may not all have been the gorgeous garments of the portraits: although she enjoyed a display, her private inclination was for plain dresses.

Contemporaries spoke, often with disgust, of fashions changing every year, though the shifts were so slight that they are scarcely apparent to less sophisticated eyes nearly four centuries later. Other reasons for criticism, to Englishmen of patriotic or puritan leanings, were the constant copying of foreign fashions, and the tendency for people to dress above their station. There were other objections. The Rev. William Harrison complained that he found it hard to distinguish between men and women in London. "Women are become men", he said, "and men transformed into monsters".

COSMETICS

In almost any age, the things that women do to themselves for the sake of what the age regards as beauty make horrifying reading. Cosmetics in Elizabethan England were used by men as well as women. They were home-made and crude. The ideal of female beauty was a white face in which eyes and mouth were strongly marked, and to achieve this effect some desperate means were employed. The skin was whitened with white lead.

was sometimes deliberately roughened so that the colour would hold. Washing in a mixture of asses milk and rose-water was thought to keep the skin white. Sun tans were avoided if possible, whiteness being in favour, although the bleaching action of the sun on hair was appreciated.

Making-up or "painting" the face attracted strong criticism, and not only from Puritans—although religious reasons were sometimes advanced against the practice. Woe unto those, said one such writer, upon whose face God shall look in anger because it is not the face he gave them! Samuel Purchas, better known as the less worthy successor of Hakluyt as chronicler of English voyages, deplored the vanity of women as worse than wicked. These warnings of doom had little effect on ladies in high society. The Queen in

a poison the long-term result of which was the opposite of that achieved in the short run. When the complexion was badly marked (perhaps by smallpox) the face was treated with sublimate of mercury, the effect of which was exactly that of flaying the skin. It was hoped that the new layer, when it grew, would be better than the old. To keep the teeth white, they were brushed (the "brush" was a frayed stick) with abrasives like brick dust: again, the effect was brilliant for a time but ultimately disastrous. The eyes were outlined with kohl and belladonna, a poison obtained from Deadly Nightshade.

Not everyone adopted such dire methods. A milder way of removing freckles, said to be effective, was to tap the sap of birch trees and apply that to the skin. A mixture of honey, vinegar and wine, boiled together, would whiten the teeth, according to the author of *Delights for Ladies* (1608). Sorrel juice removed stains from the hands.

The hair was artifically curled, sometimes supported on wire frames, and oiled and scented: it may have looked and even smelt attractive, but it was almost never washed and was probably full of lice. Hair was often dyed and many ladies wore wigs (in the Queen's case, a necessity). The eyebrows were plucked out with tweezers and painted in to make a neater, arching line. Lips and cheeks were reddened with cochineal, and the skin

her later years made up her face so thickly, it was said, that she was compelled to maintain an unmoving expression for fear of cracking the layers of paint.

BEARDS

The fashion among men for short hair and beards began in the reign of Henry VIII and lasted throughout the 16th century. By 1600, however, gentlemen were wearing their hair longer, so that it fell well over the ears. Beards remained in fashion until the middle of the 17th century.

The beard of a fashionable Elizabethan gentleman was most frequently small and pointed, and complemented by a moustache. Shakespeare himself, in the representations we have of him, is often shown in this fashion. But individual barbers cultivated individual fashions; men's hair was curled with hot irons in the same way as women's and held in place by some type of lacquer.

These was a good deal of variety, and hair and beard were often dyed. Some wore their hair cut short, almost like a crew cut; some grew it long, some curled, some straight. The old "pudding-basin" cut—a solid fringe all the way round—was still seen occasionally, perhaps mostly in the country. Beards too : if a man has a lean and straight face, wrote Harrison, then a Marquess Otto cut will make it broad and large ("like a glover's paring knife" as Mistress Quickly says). If he has a face like a plate, a long, slender beard will make it look narrower; if he looks like a weasel,

he should leave much hair on his cheeks which will make him look as "grim as a goose" (though why this effect should be considered desirable the writer does not say). Some beards were shaved to below the chin, "like the Turk", some were cut very short, some were round like a bush, and some grew long. Elderly men often wore no beard at all, according to Harrison. Moustaches were similarly treated: some were encouraged like a vine to grow out to the ears; others were cut down to the lip, in the Italian manner.

Elizabethans were extremely fussy about their hair. Almost all men wore beards, but they could be trimmed in an endless variety of ways, as can be seen from the portraits shown here.

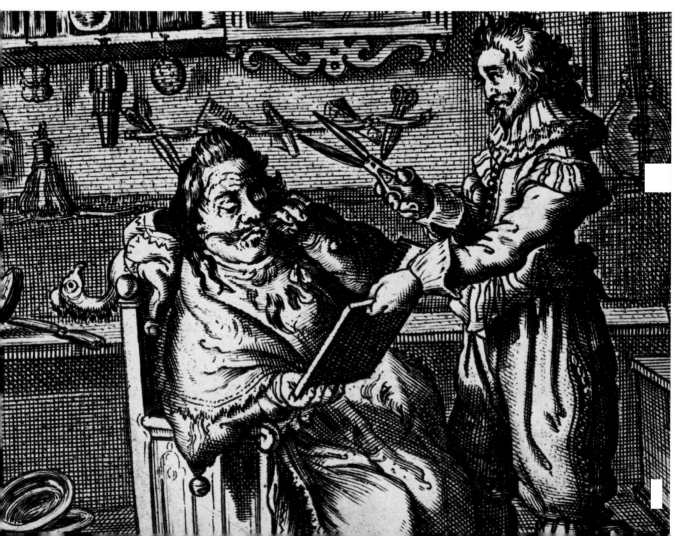

HATS, MASKS AND LADIES' ACCOUTREMENTS

It has been suggested that an age in which men normally wear beards is likely also to be an age of large hats. At any rate, Elizabethans liked hats, especially hats of a highly decorative kind, and both men and women wore them indoors as well as out. In the early years of the reign, high-crowned beaver hats, often with a dyed ostrich feather in the band, were coming into fashion. Tricorn hats of ermine or squirrel fur were also favoured, but older types were still common, such as the soft, roundish hat with curling brim that seems to have derived originally from Spain and looked something like a collapsible bowler, or the stiff-crowned hat with a short, level brim. Elderly men commonly wore a round, embroidered cap, which their sons too might wear in the house. Craftsmen and apprentices wore plain woollen caps or bonnets, or a flat, brimmed hat. Soldiers wore a round, brimless cap with tapering crown.

Hats of all sorts were increasingly worn by women in the late 16th century, and not only by married women, as formerly. The hair itself was frequently adorned with jewels. Hoods could still be seen frequently, but they were becoming less fashionable. In general, hats for women followed men's styles. A stiff-crowned hat with a short curly brim was popular by about 1590, and so was the wide, round, flat hat with drooping feather, worn at a jaunty angle. But there were many others, and it was becoming accepted for ladies to choose the hat that suited the shape of their face.

More traditional headwear was a type of cap or bonnet, silk-embroidered, which could be worn under a hat; or a lace-embroidered coif, which was tied under the chin or pinned to the hair. The hood-like caps of an earlier period, such as the "gothic"-framed type worn by Catherine of Aragon, could still be seen, at least in country districts, and so could the heart-shaped hood favoured by Mary Queen of Scots.

Legislation designed to assist manufacturers adjured the wives of citizens to wear woollen caps, sometimes called "statute caps", but like all laws which attempt to obstruct the implacable march of fashion, it was probably more honoured in the breach than in the observance. According to the traveller Fynes Morison, beaver hats were adopted when the wearing of raised silk caps was forbidden.

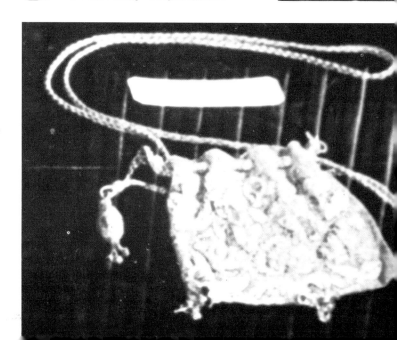

On special occasions, hats of taffeta were worn, but felt was the usual material for everyday wear. Hats of velvet or silk were made on a leather base. Straw hats were worn only by the poor; they were simple, conical objects, made to keep the sun off the wearer's head and neck.

Silk masks were sometimes worn by ladies, ostensibly for reasons wholly practical. White skin being in fashion, the face had to be protected against the effects of sunlight, and indoors masks were allegedly worn to keep off the heat from the fire. A great lady mixing with the throng on some public occasion might wear a mask to protect her identity although, like darkened windows in a private car, one may suspect this expedient encouraged more curiosity than it diverted.

Fashionable ladies often carried muffs and fans which, like so much else, came from Italy. Several portraits of the Queen show her holding an ostrich-feather fan (Sir Francis Drake gave her such a fan), and by about 1590 (perhaps earlier) folding fans were in use. Clearly, such fans were mainly decorative, though humbler folks than Elizabeth may well have found them useful for keeping off flies. The Queen once accidentally dropped a silver fan into the moat of some great house she was visiting (she had 26 others, so it was no great loss). Muffs were not the big fur bundles of Victorian times; they were chiefly decorative, and were often made of embroidered silk.

Ladies also carried various objects hanging on a chain from their girdle. The commonest was a small mirror, which was sometimes incorporated in a fan. Miniature portraits of loved ones, or more practical objects like keys, a pomander, a purse, or a silver ornament called a "chatelaine" combining these and other items, might be carried.

No lady was properly dressed without gloves (more strictly gauntlets), which still served a number of social functions unconnected with the protection of the hands: for instance, a man might still wear his lady's glove as a token in his hat. Gloves were frequently given as presents, and thus were highly ornamented—jeweled, fringed, embroidered, and sometimes scented.

Jewelry was worn by both sexes. Jewels were sewn on to clothes, hats, shoes. Buttons, more often used as decorations than as fasteners, were often simply jewels: the Queen was once given 60 gold and enamelled buttons in the shape of crowns, each set with a pearl. Among other objects in the form of, or set with, jewels, were lockets and brooches, necklaces and earrings, buckles, toothpicks—in fact anything remotely suitable. Strings of pearls and beads of black glass were sometimes employed to dress a lady's hair.

There were some odd transitory fashions in jewelry. Ear "strings", stretching from the ear lobe to the neck and adorned with jewels, were worn by men for a short period.

Both sexes wore rings, sometimes several of them. Occasionally, they were attached to the wrist by a cord, as in the portrait of Ann Seymour (in the Cheltenham Museum and Art Gallery). Seal rings, with a design cut in agate, were useful means of identification: Shakespeare's plays include several examples of messengers giving rings to reassure the recipient of the authenticity of the message.

Watches, worn on a string around the neck or from the girdle, appeared during the 16th century. The earliest portrait in Britain that shows a watch being worn in this way is Hans Eworth's painting (at Holyrood Palace) of the young Lord Darnley (father of James I) in 1563. The watch in question was probably gold, decorated with blue enamel. By modern standards, such watches did not keep very strict time. They did not presume to indicate minutes, let alone seconds. However, they should not be dismissed as exclusively ornamental or amusing. In the 16th century no one wanted to know *exactly* what the time was.

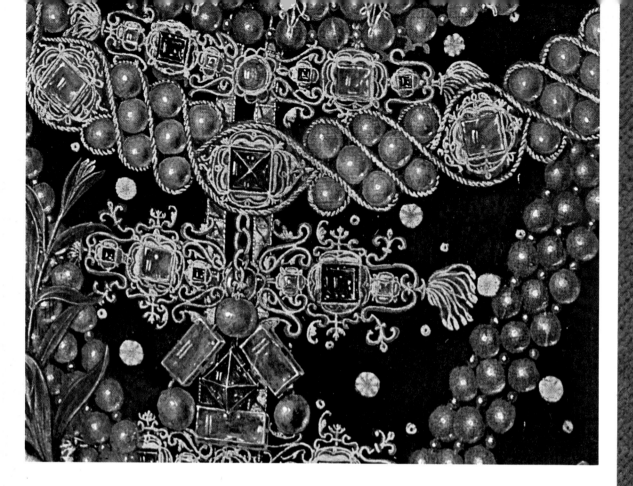

"HEMPEN HOMESPUN" (Cheap clothes)

The main evidence for the dress of both men and women in Elizabethan England comes from portraits. Not only are these almost always of the upper strata of society, the subjects, from the Queen downwards, are inevitably wearing their best clothes. Naturally, there is little direct evidence of what poor folk wore, day in, day out, in the stable, the field, the shop and the kitchen.

The fabulous dresses of the Queen's wardrobe would have astonished the country housewife, who commonly wore a simple cloth gown, though as time went on the extravagance of court dress began to have an effect right down the social scale and in counties far from London.

An inventory of the clothes of a peasant farmer, renting land worth £1 a year, and his wife survives from the early years of the reign. The farmer's wife had two gowns, of which the best was worth 10 shillings (£0.50), three kirtles, two petticoats, a silver brooch and several caps and kerchiefs. Her husband had a gown worth 5 shillings, a doublet and jerkin worth 7 shillings and a cheap, canvas doublet (as worn by servants), two pairs of hose, two shirts, a coat with sleeves and a cap.

The list may be incomplete since several items are missing, but it would certainly have been longer and more lavish half a century later when poor people "carried on their backs the greater part of what they earned" and, according to Philip Stubbes, every poor cottager's daughter had a taffeta hat. Leather doublets were common but perhaps reserved for special occasions. Poor country people wore tunics of fustian, which had knee-length skirts, together with loose breeches or hose and cloth (not knitted) stockings. Sometimes they wore leggings, made of strips of cloth wound around the leg. A poor countryman in a sheepskin doublet, recorded in contemporary verse, wore "upon his head a filthy, greasy hat, that had a hole ate through it by a rat". He carried a plain leather pouch, wore cloth stockings, knitted hose, and hobnailed shoes. His whole outfit, the poet calculated, was not worth a shilling.

At that level of society, women's dress was little different from men's. She would wear a coarse woollen gown of ankle length, perhaps with a linen apron. Below the gown was nothing except a smock—in cold weather, with any luck, two or three smocks. The head was covered by a linen cap, covering the hair, unlike the caps of more prosperous ladies who liked to display some of their hair.

The finery worn by the nobility was studded with precious stones. And, as the pieces reproduced here show, Elizabethan jewelry was exquisitely made.

7. FOOD, DRINK AND TOBACCO

FOOD

It is usually assumed that the Elizabethans ate only two meals a day. The substantial English breakfast of earlier—and later—times was apparently out of favour, perhaps because people did not rise so early. Ordinary working people, however, do seem to have had a solid if simple breakfast, and we read of the Queen's maids—not, presumably, a notably greedy group—taking a breakfast of beef, bread and beer. In short, the alleged neglect of breakfast seems to have been confined to a rather small number of people.

The main meal of the day was eaten at noon or before. Supper, in the late afternoon, tended to be a simpler form of the midday dinner. The arrangement of courses would be strange to us. There was a tendency for each course to be a meal in itself, and the balance of savoury and sweet that we are accustomed to was absent. On a fish-eating day, for instance, one course of fish dishes would be followed by another, and it is not clear what, if any, distinction there was between the two.

A remarkable number of dishes were served. At one, admittedly very grand meal described by a contemporary, the guests were able to partake of the following: roast beef, salted beef, veal, leg of mutton, turkey (a recent innovation), boiled capon, chicken with leeks, partridge, pheasant, larks, quails, snipe, and woodcock. So much for meat and poultry. There was also fish: salmon, sole, turbot, whiting, eel and pike, lobster, crayfish and shrimps. There were more delicate meats—rabbit, young hares and marrow served on toast—and vegetables: artichokes, turnips, green peas, cucumbers and olives, plus salads of several kinds. For dessert there was quince pie, almond tart, various fruit tarts and fresh strawberries with cream, besides several kinds of cheese.

Of course, the guests at such a meal were not expected to sample every dish. They chose what they fancied. Several dishes were returned to the kitchens untouched. At the dining table, however, one could see the extravagance of the period given full play. And not only in the number of dishes provided at a single meal. Some recipes were so weird and exotic that one suspects they were never meant to be eaten but designed merely to make a sensational effect, like the boar's head or similar centrepiece that was brought on at the beginning of a meal. No expense was spared, and at least the servants were pleased if much luxurious food came back to the kitchen.

Harrison, in whom patriotism is sometimes at war with honesty, insists that the English were not particularly large eaters. They needed to eat more than other nations, he asserts, because of the effect on their stomachs of the cool northern latitude. But he ruins this already doubtful case by attacking the Scots for gross gourmandizing, quite forgetting that since they live even farther north, they would need to eat more than the English.

Meals, for the well-to-do at least, consisted mainly of meat, including game and wildfowl of many sorts that would not be eaten today in most civilized countries. Fish, including shellfish (especially oysters) was also eaten in quantity. It was compulsory on Fridays and during Lent (when meat was most scarce), a purely political rule designed to keep the fishing industry, which was the navy's nursery, prosperous. Most houses had a pond where fish were kept, and the sea is never more than 75 miles away wherever you live in England. Eating fish was certainly no hardship in a rich household: salmon figured largely, along with haddock and herrings; even sturgeon was available.

Most of the food eaten in Elizabethan times

The kitchen, whether in a great country house or a humbler dwelling, was always an important place. And the quantities of provisions used were large, even for a picnic (below).

Facing, an Elizabethan kitchen, as seen in the middle of the famous painting of a rural gathering: The feast at Berstmonday. Bottom, a memorable banquet from the life of Sir Henry Unton (third from left).

would be familiar today, although we have some foods that they never knew. The greatest differences between eating then and eating now were in the realm of costs. A whole leg of mutton cost one or two shillings in the late 16th century, but a pound of sugar cost about the same.

This was of course a matter of supply and demand: sugar was not easily come by, and the population had a sweet tooth. Cakes, biscuits and comfits of many kinds were in great demand: a box of Naples biscuits sold for half-a-crown (2.5 shillings), and marzipan was a particular favourite. Everything that could be candied was candied.

But fresh fruit was also much appreciated, both home-grown and imported. Most of the fruit grown in England today was familiar 400 years ago. Strawberries were a long-time favourite, though raspberries had only recently begun to be enjoyed, perhaps as a result of some improvement in the stock. Gooseberries, introduced in the reign of Henry VIII, had become common by the end of the century. Of imported fruits, the commonest were oranges and lemons. The former were special favourites and, at a guess, are mentioned in contemporary literature more than any other fruit.

DRINK

Nearly everyone drank either wine or beer with his meals. The glass (the preferred drinking vessel, though pewter or earthenwere were still common) was not placed on the table but on the adjacent sideboard or buffet. If and when the diner required a drink, he would be handed a glass by the servant, who would replace it when enough had been drunk. If a second drink was required in the course of the meal, a second glass was provided. Various explanations have been put forward of this custom. It seems unlikely that people were so finicky as to demand a fresh glass with each drink. Another explanation, that it was designed to prevent drunkenness, seems a little more likely although, like the present licensing laws which restrict the opening time of British bars and public houses, it might have had an opposite effect by encouraging the drinker to drink as much as possible while he had the chance. It may have prevented breakages: glasses were expensive and meals could become riotous. Or it may just have been simpler to take the glass to the jug rather than the other way around.

Wine was preferred much heavier and sweeter than would appeal to a modern palate. The favourite tipple of that mighty drinker, Sir John Falstaff, was sack, a generic name for fortified wines of the type that would now be mostly called sherry. He was able to purchase two gallons of sack for less than six shillings at the Boar's Head Tavern. It was, of course, imported (mainly from Spain), but so was most other wine; English wine production, then as now, was more of a hobby than a business and it was often made from fruit other than grapes. A native wine made from raspberries was sometimes drunk with enthusiasm.

The best red wine came from Gascony, which had once been an English possession. In spite of the current preference for Burgundy, the English

have, traditionally, been claret drinkers for that reason. Rhenish wine was also popular, and some wines were imported from Italy, Greece, Portugal and the Canary Islands.

Wine was often mulled and spiced, and so was beer. An orange stuck with cloves was sometimes steeped in a barrel of beer. Such spices as mace (much used in the 16th century), nutmeg and even sage were also added to beer, or to cider, that characteristically English drink made from apples which, then as now, was made mainly in the south and south-west of the country. (According to the contemporary historian, William Camden, it was a wretched, counterfeit wine which caused wind.)

It is impossible to be certain what these various drinks tasted like, for a claret of the 1580s was no doubt very different from the vintage of today. There were also many drinks with exotic names which we may call cocktails. One or two recipes for these have come down to us: mix together cinammon, white ginger, cloves, nutmeg, "grains of Paradise" and pepper and steep in spirits of wine for a week. Then add it to a bowl of wine which, with the further addition of a flask of ale, became a drink called "Gossip's Cup". No doubt it loosened the tongue.

Beer was probably much stronger then. Certainly, 17th century beer glasses seem very small by comparison with the pint mug of today. But there were various types of beer, some stronger than others. At least one foreign visitor, the Duke of Württemburg in the 1590s, preferred English beer to French wine, which disagreed with him. The Queen is said to have shared his preference.

Several contemporaries insist that drunkenness was uncommon. This may to some extent be a wishful judgment, as drunkenness was generally frowned on—not only by Puritans. But the Queen is said to have been much amused when an actor in a masque put on for her entertainment made a muddle of his lines through being fuddled with drink, which suggests that she saw nothing very disgraceful or even unusual in such an incident. Pure spirits—*aqua vitae*—were not often drunk, and then, as a rule, for medicinal purposes only.

High spirits on Christmas Eve...
Facing, a distiller's plant.

TOBACCO

Popular legend ascribes to Sir Walter Raleigh the doubtful honour of introducing tobacco to England. A story is told of how his servant coming into the room one day was horrified to see smoke gushing from his master. He hastily seized hold of a bucket of water and threw it over him to put out the fire.

While that anecdote is well substantiated, it seems that tobacco was known in England before Raleigh had the chance to import it, though he surely helped to make it popular. Like the sweet potato (not the Virginia potato which is also traditionally credited to Raleigh), it seems to have been introduced about 1565. Writing only eight years later, Harrison remarks that "in these days, the taking in of the smoke of the Indian herb called Tobacco by an instrument formed like a little ladle, whereby it passeth from the mouth into the head and stomach, is greatly taken up and used in England". Apparently it was considered an aid to health, especially "against diseases engendered in the lungs" (Quoted *Shakespeare's England* II page 141).

Originally taken up by courtiers always prone to exotic new habits, it spread rapidly. There were said to be thousands of tobacco-sellers in London by the end of the century, and a common pipe was often provided for the customers of an inn. Women smoked it as well as men, using longstemmed pipes allegedly (none seems to have survived) with silver bowls, and at first, like all fads, smoking was a public activity. Its solitary comforts were discovered later.

Several foreign commentators remarked on the popularity of tobacco in England (though it was not cheap: as much as five shillings an ounce in 1589). Oddly enough, Shakespeare never mentions it: perhaps he was a non-smoker who, like many others, disapproved of smoking. There is at least one example of a will revoking a legacy if the recipient should stoop to the vice of smoking, and the most famous opponent of the habit was none other than King James I. In a memorable pamphlet written in 1604, James described it as "a custom loathsome to the eye, hateful to the nose, harmful to the brain, dangerous to the lungs, and in the black stinking fume thereof nearest resembling the horrible Stygian smoke of the pit that is bottomless".

James' attack was not published until long after his death, but a minor pamphlet war was waged by the supporters and opponents of smoking in the 17th century. "Work for Chimney Sweepers" in 1601 accused tobacco of causing all manner of unpleasant conditions and diseases, while "A Defender of Tobacco", which appeared soon afterwards, insisted that, on the contrary, smoking was good for you.

The smoking of tobacco began during the reign of Elizabeth, and spread very quickly.

The pipe of the gentleman shown opposite has visibly upset his life and children. Below, a smoking party.

8. THE COUNTRY

ON THE FARM

In spite of many changes such as the growing of hops (formerly imported from the Low Countries), farming in general had not changed fundamentally since the Middle Ages. For the majority, subsistence farming was the rule; those farming for profit remained a small, though growing minority. Bacon was being too optimistic when he said in 1592 that England could be a net exporter of food, though wheat was exported in good years. The open-field system, the most characteristic agricultural system of the Middle Ages though by no means universal, was still widespread in parts of the Midlands and eastern England. Typically (but with numerous variations) there were three great fields, cultivated on a three-year system: wheat, barley or rye one year, oats, beans or peas the next, fallow the third. No clovers or artificial grasses were grown.

Each field was divided into strips, and every man held land in all three fields: if he had 15 acres, he had five acres in each field. But his three pieces of land were themselves divided into strips of perhaps half an acre each, so that everyone had some of the good land and some of the poor land in each field. There was also grazing and waste land held in common.

The disadvantages of this system are obvious. Apart from the waste of land and the dangerous dependence on a small number of crops, improvement or experiment was virtually impossible. For example, winter crops like turnips could not be grown by an enterprising farmer because, after harvest, the field was used for common pasture until sowing time came round in the spring; his winter roots, in the unprotected strips, would not have lasted long. Nor was there any point in keeping one's strip clear of weeds if one had a lazy neighbour who let what Shakespeare called "hateful docks, rough thistles, kecksies, burrs" flourish freely.

Farm animals were in general scrawny beasts, forced to look after themselves to a considerable degree, but there were some improvements and innovations apparent. The horse particularly was

A Countryman

Left, the English countryside... the photo at lower left shows a scene from the Midlands.

85

Two sections of the superb Sheldon Tapestry, from Hatfield House, depict the pleasures of the country life in summer.

becoming a more specialized creature. The English "Great Horse", a descendant of the heavy medieval war horse and the ancestor of the modern shire horse, was beginning to play an important part on the farm. There was also a demand for lighter, faster horses, something approaching the modern hunter, although the fox was still regarded as inferior quarry and horse-racing had not yet acquired the popularity it was to enjoy in the second half of the 17th century. Horses, the best of which came from the north, received special treatment: they were given better-quality hay than that given to oxen.

In general, oxen were still preferred as draught animals (in a few places, oxen were still drawing a plough in the 19th century). They were cheaper to keep than horses, they were tougher and less vulnerable to disease, and when their working days were over, they were eatable. For nothing, not even the Common Market, has been able to persuade the English that horse flesh is fit for anything except dogfood.

Animals were not bred for meat, largely because meat was not always their main product. Although the English ate a lot of mutton, sheep were bred

for wool and, secondarily, for leather; meat came a long way third. Cows were kept for milk, of course, while pigs were kept for bacon, probably the only meat eaten regularly by the poorer classes. Rather than fat, animals had to be lean and fit, for they often had to roam long distances to feed themselves. Pigs were fed on beech mast and acorns as long as they were available. One contemporary writer on farming regarded a sow as more profitable than a cow.

In these conditions, with everyone's animals mixing on common pasture or waste land, it was obviously impossible to organize breeding, and it has been suggested that farm animals were actually declining in quality owing to promiscuous interbreeding and chronic disease. There were virtually no breeds of cattle, or other animals, in quite the modern sense, rather a vast number of local breeds. Individually, they were certainly much smaller than modern animals, probably little more than half their weight.

Apart from breeding stock, most animals were still slaughtered in the autumn—the first or second week of November—and the meat was salted for the winter. Probably many people knew the flavour of salted meat better than fresh.

ENCLOSURES

One way of improving farming was by "enclosure"— the fencing in of fields by a single owner or tenant. It was no coincidence that the county of Kent, where enclosed fields had long been customary, was famous for the prosperity of its farmers. (Kent owed something also to its proximity to the capital: it was the "kitchen garden", still more the orchard, of London.) There was nothing new in enclosures: they had been going on in a small way for many years as part of the improvement in farming methods. But from the late 15th century, enclosure was, or seemed to be, greatly accelerated. To some extent this was part of the gradual change from a medieval to a modern society, from a society in which land meant status and power (in the number of vassals it supported) to a society in which land was valued primarily for financial profits.

Enclosure could be of several different kinds. It might be nothing more than a yeoman farmer reclaiming a piece of waste land. It might be a change from an open-field system to a system of enclosed, arable fields, which permitted far more versatility in crops. Or it might be the enclosure of arable land, or of common land, for sheep pasture. No one could object to the reclamation of useless waste, nor to a more efficient way of using arable land. What caused all the trouble was enclosure for sheep.

There were obvious advantages in a change from arable to sheep. Sheep required less labour and wool happened to be particularly profitable in the early 16th century. But there were concomitant disadvantages. Any tenant farmer whose tenure could be broken was likely to find himself dispossessed. Wage labourers were left without work, and perhaps also lost some valuable minor perquisites when common land was—with or without legal justification—fenced in.

An angry outcry was raised against enclosures, which were blamed for the desertion of whole villages and for the serious unemployment problem —and indeed for all agrarian problems. Thomas More spoke of "sheep eating men" and his somewhat hysterical image was eagerly adopted by other propagandists: in contemporary writings, the Tudor sheep sounds more like a man-eating tiger. A famous anonymous commentary on the state of England published in the 1580s (but written a generation earlier) comments: "where corn of all sorts and beasts of all kinds were reared in former times, now there is nothing but sheep. And instead of some 100 or 200 persons that had their livings thereon, now there are but three or four shepherds and the master who have a living there". (*A Discourse of the Common Weal*... O.U.P. 1893, page 48, wording simplified). There were several peasant risings in which enclosures figured prominently among the grievances stated.

The government under the grandfather and father of Elizabeth had attempted to prevent enclosure for pasture by legislation, and Elizabeth's government followed the same policy. The conversion of ploughland to pasture was forbidden by an act of 1563 and, although this act was repealed in 1593, the restrictions had to be reimposed five years later in response to popular pressure. The situation was easier in Shakespeare's time than it had been in the first half of the century, partly because the profits of sheep farming were declining, thus making it a less attractive alternative. And the government was probably more concerned with soothing public discontent than with any realistically adjuged economic trend.

People had become accustomed to blaming enclosures for everything. Nowadays the English blame incompetent managers or stubborn shop stewards for all their economic troubles; in the 16th century they blamed greedy landlords and their sheep. Elizabethan people could not understand why things should be expensive though

In Elizabethan, as in earlier times, a special kind of aura attached to the pastoral life. Below, rustic dwelling, with its enclosure.

plentiful. We know more about inflation than they did and can see that the trouble was an over-abundance of bullion resulting in a fall in the value of money. But the ordinary citizen watching a play at the Globe Theatre or drinking a glass of wine at the inn placed the blame firmly on sheep.

In spite of enclosure for sheep, there was no fall in food production. On the contrary, the country had a surplus in good years. Enclosures may have had something to do with the growing shortage of timber, but they clearly cannot be blamed for a shortage of food. We now know that the complaints about enclosures were greatly exaggerated. In the east Midlands, where enclosure was most frequent, the total of land enclosed was about 6 per cent. In East Anglia, where the peasants led by Robert Kett had risen in revolt in 1549, it was much less. In the 18th century, when enclosure went on at a far greater pace, roughly half the agricultural land was still under the open-field system. Although enclosure certainly did cause severe hardship (the cold statistics of historians should not be allowed to suppress the cries of real distress), there were other problems behind the agrarian crisis, most of them admittedly connected, like enclosure for sheep pasture, with the gradual change from a feudal economy to a capitalist economy. Shakespeare himself was engaged in a local conflict over enclosure. A man named Combe wished to enclose common land in Stratford and had to obtain the agreement of Shakespeare, who held certain rights in the land. Shakespeare agreed to be bought out, but the Stratford corporation strongly resisted Combe's plans. The matter went to law and the Lord Chief Justice gave judgment for the corporation.

Markets and fairs, where the peasant women would take their produce and the farmers their sheep, often lent themselves to general merrymaking.

FAIRS

Most of the necessities of life in Elizabeth's time—food, drink, clothes, even tools and utensils—were made at home. What was not produced in the household was acquired from travelling craftsmen or bought in the local weekly market. What could not be obtained in the market was bought at a regional fair.

The fair was like a market, but usually much larger and with a greater degree of competition among vendors than could be found in a market town. Fairs were held less frequently than markets, some only once a year. Bargains might be struck at one fair and the sale concluded at the next, as sometimes happens in modern international fairs, like the Frankfurt Book Fair. Some transactions might be prolonged over three or four successive fairs in different parts of the country.

Fairs were ancient, predating the towns, which regarded them without enthusiasm as competitors. Eventually, of course, the towns superseded them completely, but in Elizabethan times fairs were still going strong.

The most famous was the fair at Stourbridge, held in a large field near Cambridge during the last three weeks in September, i.e. after the crop had been harvested. But there were many other big fairs, at places like Bristol, Lynn, Boston and, of course, St. Bartholomew's fair in London, made famous by Ben Jonson's play. There were also fairs for specialised purposes in various parts of the country, selling (for example) horses, or cheeses. The east coast port of Yarmouth had an annual herring fair.

The fair was like a temporary city, with the clothiers, goldsmiths, butchers, fishmongers arranged in rows of stalls like the shops in the London streets. But a big fair like Stourbridge would also attract foreign merchants, selling silks and spices from Italy, leather and furs from Germany and the Baltic, wine from Gascony, and copper and brass from Dinant, which gave to English the term "dinanderie"—small objects of brass.

The London merchants had tried without success to strangle the Stourbridge fair which, though 60 miles from London, was near enough to attract London customers. Many of them found it more profitable to take part. In the 17th century, people used to travel from the capital to Stourbridge in hired cabs. Stewards from the great houses in the country for over 50 miles round about where there, laying in a year's supplies. Anyone in the region with money to spend would manage to visit Stourbridge fair.

Even if they did not buy, there was amusement and instruction. Country bumpkins could see the latest fashions; musicians, jugglers and keepers of performing animals could pick up a few pence; confidence tricksters and pickpockets could ply their trades with advantage. There was much to eat and drink: so much that these occupations seemed to be the primary purpose of some fairs where, as William Harrison complained, there was "little else bought and sold than good drink, pies and pedlars' trash". Bartholomew's Fair seems to have been a little like this in the 17th century: "a noisy gathering of toyshops and gingerbread stalls, of pig-women and quack-doctors, of showmen and balladmongers, of horse-dealers and pickpockets" (George Unwin in *Shakespeare's England* O.U.P. 1916, pages 313-14). Bartholomew's Fair was a curious mixture, characteristic of the age: the mayor and city aldermen in their ceremonial robes of office were likely to get mixed up with a pair of yokels having a wrestling match or a crowd of boys chasing rabbits.

9. TOWN LIFE

LONDON

Today, there is little left of London as Elizabeth knew it. Riots and fires—especially the Great Fire of 1666—have swept most of it away, though there are notable exceptions, like William the Conqueror's White Tower, now entering its tenth century. And to those prepared to look closely, more relics of the past appear. It is said that Cardinal Wolsey's cellars are still in existence somewhere below Whitehall, which was once named York Place after Wolsey himself (he was archbishop of York).

Although London had spread far beyond its ancient walls, it was still a single city, separate from the neighbouring city of Westminster and far removed from the numerous villages which have long since been incorporated in Greater London. It was impressively large, the largest city in northern Europe and on its way to becoming the largest city in the world. No other town in England was one-tenth its size, and it dominated the country more thoroughly than it does now.

The twin cities of London and Westminster were linked by the River Thames, London's great artery, up whose reaches sailed the ships of many

nations. The Thames made London—the city had grown on the site of a prehistoric settlement at the place nearest the sea at which the river could be forded—and it was still the main highway of London. For it was easier to travel by river than through the narrow, crowded and dirty streets.

Yet the city was mainly confined to the north bank of the river. Southwark, on the south bank, was filled with inns, brothels, and places of entertainment, including the first permanent custom-built theatres, erected as far as was practical from the restrictions of an increasingly stuffy city government. Shakespeare himself lived nearby, in Bankside, for some years.

Southwark, and the main highways to the south, were reached by London Bridge, the city's pride. It was worthy to be numbered among the wonders of the world, thought the traveller Fynes Morison, and another writer remarked that there was nothing in the world to compare it with, discounting the Ponte Vecchio, not to mention surviving Roman bridges. So great a structure with its narrow arches and thick piers, which, according to tradition, rested on woolsacks, was a serious hindrance to navigation. The construction of water-mills to grind corn in some of the arches (a characteristic piece

London in the rain... Below, the town-houses of the nobility along the Strand, overlooking the Thames.

of social irresponsibility, like the Nottinghamshire man who gaily sunk a coal mine in the public highway) helped not at all. It was built over for most of its length, so that walking along it, the pedestrian seemed to be not on a bridge but on an excessivly dark (the buildings were joined at the top) city street. There were several clear spaces, at one of which a drawbridge allowed tall-masted ships to pass.

The two greatest buildings in London were St. Paul's Cathedral and the Tower. The Tower, in spite of its sinister reputation, had many uses. As described by John Stow in his *Survey of London* (1598), it was "a citadel, to defend or command the city; a royal place for meetings and treaties, a state prison for the most dangerous offenders, the only place of coinage for all England at this time, the armory for warlike provision, the Treasury of the ornaments and jewels of the Crown, and general conserver of most records of the King's Courts of Justice at Westminster". (Quoted *Shakespeare's England* II, 157).

St. Paul's Cathedral, denuded of its spire by lightning in 1561, served all the social functions of a medieval cathedral and was familiar with the same kind of behaviour that made Jesus clear out the Synagogue. The main aisle was a kind of capital common room, where the freshest gossip was exchanged and the latest developments at court

St. Paul's Cathedral towers over the city.

were disseminated among a wider public. In the cathedral you could buy beer or bread, you could hire a workman or consult a lawyer; you could even stable your horse. The city government forbade such practices in 1554, but to judge from the evidence of Ben Jonson's plays, the situation had not changed half a century later.

Rebuilding was going on constantly, and the most significant new building in Shakespeare's time was the Royal Exchange, founded by the greatest financial expert of the age, Sir Thomas Gresham (the dictum, "bad money drives out good", which in England is known as Gresham's Law is actually much older). It was named "Royal" after Queen Elizabeth's visit to the newly erected building in 1571 and, for the mercantile interests, it was soon performing the function that St. Paul's Cathedral fulfilled for lawyers and others.

London was, above all, a merchant city, proud of its ancient privileges secured by medieval charter, "a large, excellent and mighty city in business", as the Duke of Württemberg said in 1602, where "most of the inhabitants are employed in buying and selling merchandise, and trading in almost every corner of the world, since the river is most useful and convenient for this purpose..." The residential streets were lined with substantial merchants' houses, while the rich halls of the city companies occupied (along with the ubiquitous churches) the most convenient sites. London was more of a city, in our modern sense, than any other town, a place quite foreign to the average Englishman, who was essentially still a countryman. When the lord of some distant, rural manor appeared in Fleet Street, then a showplace for conjurors, puppet shows, freaks and strange creatures, he was as easily distinguished as the most exotic foreigner. His clothes, voice and manner gave him away instantly. He continually stumbled in the gutters, bumped into hurrying porters, and stood under waterspouts, attracting the hungry eyes of every thief, prostitute and con-man in the vicinity. Shopkeepers, seeing him, at once hoped to sell him second-hand, faulty or stolen goods.

Parts of London were unsavoury. No honest man ventured out after dark unaccompanied; even in daylight he did not go into the area of Whitefriars, or Alsatia, where criminals retained a safe refuge until the end of the 17th century. And less notorious districts were far from peaceful. Hemmed in by the crowding, overhanging buildings

(no wonder the city burned so well), splashed by carts and carriages (when they were not jamming the street), his nose assaulted by stinks and his ears by a deafening hubbub of shopkeepers advertising their wares, balladmongers singing the latest hits, citizens shouting and cursing, and bells clanging, the passing traveller was hard put to retain his equanimity even if he escaped the attentions of the pickpockets, drunks and other undesirable persons who frequented the streets of the overcrowded capital.

For all that, London had its pleasants aspects. There were the grand houses of merchants like Sir Thomas Gresham, who did not scorn to live in Bishopsgate, near the centre of business, and, along the river, the palaces of great nobles. There was

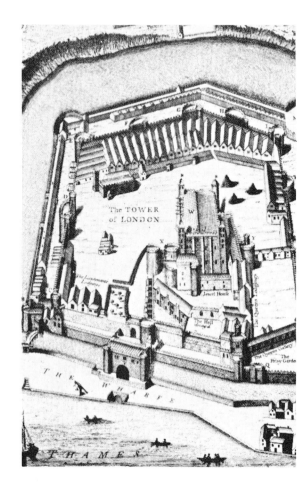

Above, Westminster Hall. The various reproductions shown below need no special comment, as they already contain the relevant place-names.

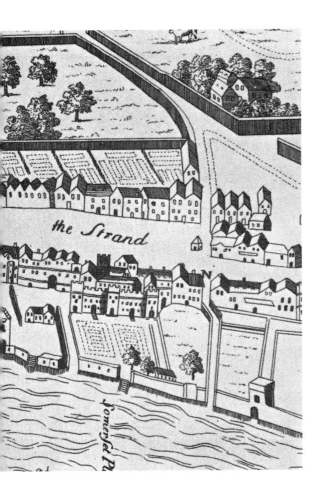

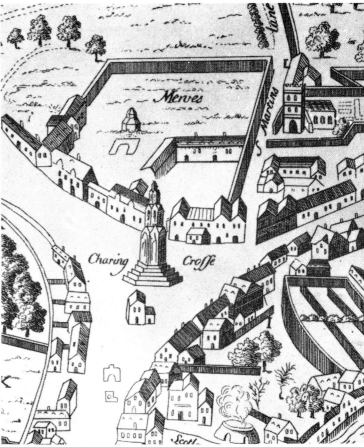

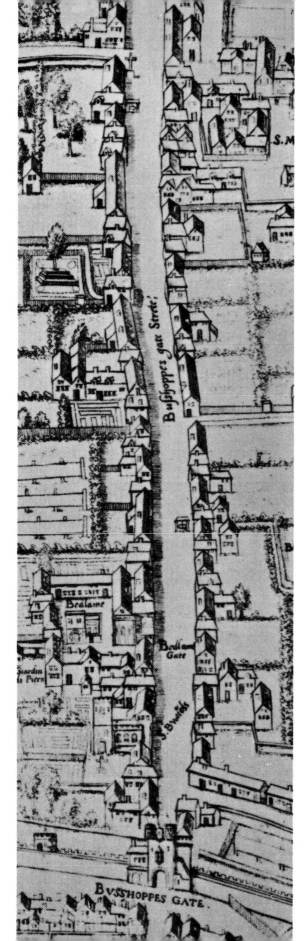

Left: typical elizabethan houses.
Facing:
A street in Smithfield, in Elizabethan times.

Below, a shop selling hats and hose.

Essex House, once the home of the Earl of Leicester, and later of his stepson, the ill-fated Earl of Essex; there was Somerset House, named after the former "Protector" of the realm, later occupied by Lord Hunsdon, the Queen's cousin who rendered her great service against the rebellious lords of the north; there was Durham House, home of the dark star of the court, Sir Walter Raleigh.

London had gardens also. The gardens of the Temple were famous for their roses, and when Sir Christopher Hatton gained possession of them from Bishop Cox (with the aid, according to tradition, of some bullying by the Queen), the Bishop retained the right of gathering 20 bushels of roses per annum. Lord Burghley, besides his other property, had a garden in the Strand. And even in London, open fields were only a short walk away.

SHOPS

In many respects, London in 1600 still bore the characteristics of a medieval town. The shops still tended to gather according to trade in a particular street, although this was slowly changing and the Londoner could buy a loaf in places other than

Bread Street, while the ironmongers had left Ironmongers Lane. According to Stow, Milk Street contained "many fair houses"; they cannot have been dairies. Stow, in his survey of London, records the peregrinations of various shops in search of more trade. West Cheap (Cheapside) was the chief shopping centre. There were gathered the goldsmith's shops, in a large block, which were one of the glories of London. They were all built alike, four storeys high, and bearing the arms of the goldsmiths' company. They made Cheapside the most splendid street in London, according to Paul Hentzner, who noted that besides vessels of silver and gold, excellent oysters could also be bought there. Perhaps that was farther east, an area once famous for its cheap restaurants though in Elizabethan times becoming popular with butchers. The cook-shops, as they were called, could be found in Thames Street, off Cheapside, which they shared with the sellers of dried fish. "Wet fish" (still the common term for fresh fish in England although "dry" fish have long disappeared) could be bought in Bridge Street, popularly known as Fish Street. Turnmill Street was the place to pick up prostitutes. Billingsgate market was not yet confined, as it is now, to the sale of fish exclusively.

The centre of the book trade was St. Paul's Churchyard, an enclosed area containing not only substantial buildings with living quarters over the shops, but also stalls of a more temporary character, something like the bookstalls of the Left Bank in Paris. The crypt of the cathedral was used as warehouse space, though that did not prevent the destruction of its contents—including, no doubt, many priceless Shakespeare folios—in the Great Fire of 1666. Booksellers were also publishers (most of Shakespeare's plays were issued from St. Paul's Churchyard) and, on occasion at least, they acted as libraries, lending books to favoured customers. Most of them sold books not published by themselves, and some dealt in foreign publications also.

Shops were not purpose-built but were merely ordinary houses adapted for the purpose of retail trade. A shopkeeper had to turn his ground-floor front room into a display area and a place to do business, while another part of the house, or perhaps the garden, was turned into a workshop. A well-to-do weaver in Exeter had to turn his hall into a bedroom at night because of shortage of space.

The studios of two different crafts-men: a jeweller and a printer.

The din of the city, different from but perhaps not less strident than the 20th-century din, was heightened by the cries of the shopkeepers standing in their doorways and expounding the quality of their goods, or merely calling "What do you lack?" with the implication that, whatever it was, their shop could supply it. In competition with them, itinerant vendors proclaimed the availability of hot cakes, fresh fish, wild herbs and other transitory delights, while others offered new books or brooms, or offered to buy second-hand articles no longer wanted by their owners.

INDUSTRY

When we speak of industry in the 16th century, we do not, of course, mean mass-production and large machines. The Elizabethans lacked the technology for mass production, and their industries were organized on the craft basis, with comparatively little division of labour and few factories (factories of a kind there were, however, sometimes housed in old monastic buildings). Nevertheless, the second half of the 16th century was a time of rapid industrial expansion, with increasing employment of capital and wage labour, and with new crafts introduced by Protestant refugees from France and the Low Countries.

It would indeed be hard to exaggerate the significance of immigrant skills in the era after the Reformation. Almost without exception, wherever we hear of new industries started or old ones revivified, we hear also of foreign craftsmen at work. When a courtier like Sir Henry Sidney decided to go in for mining, his first move was to hire a couple of German miners.

Even in the old, accustomed crafts, foreigners had an often decisive influence. In the cloth industry, for example. The domestic industry had always been strongest in the production of cheap, rough clothes; it was craftsmen from Flanders, particularly, who gave such an impetus to the production of finer fabrics. They settled mainly in the oldest region of the industry, East Anglia, where Norwich had no less than 4,000 foreign workers in 1572—about 20 per cent of the total population. Norwich, second only to London (though by a long way), was in those days a progressive place, and the attitude of the city authorities towards foreigners was comparatively enlightened. Elsewhere, they were often less than

popular. In the Essex town of Halstead, forty Dutch weavers with their families were allowed to settle. Like all immigrants, they were very industrious, and their production of fine bay cloth brought £250 a week into Halstead from London buyers. But the local yokels did not like the foreigners (they probably liked them even less for their success) and drove them out. Trade rapidly sank to about one-tenth of what it had been before, and there was much hardship among the poor. The council then endeavoured to persuade the Dutchmen to return, but they were not willing to come. Halstead remains a small place to this day.

The most striking symptom of the expansion of the cloth industry was its spread into new areas. It had formerly been chiefly confined to the towns of East Anglia, towns like Norwich or Bury St. Edmunds, and the south-east. In the early 17th century it was well-established in a far wider area—throughout the West Country, on the Welsh borders, and most notably, in Yorkshire and Lancashire. The old centres, indeed, were often in decline. Norwich was, as we have seen, prosperous enough, though by the 17th century even Norwich was seeing its rivals drawing much closer. Bury suffered through its former dependence on the immense monastic foundation whose remains still form an impressive monument, but it was also one of many older towns which were failing to gain their share of the generally increasing prosperity. This was largely due to the old, cramping regulations of the towns, the intense economic conservatism of which the guilds had been guilty; for though the craft guilds had been abolished (except in London where they were too powerful) their spirit was not dead. Often the rules were so numerous it was impossible to tell what was legal and what was not.

The cloth industry was not dependent on towns, and indeed was increasingly conducted as a cottage industry, in which the weaver (for example) would purchase his thread, weave it into cloth in his own house, and sell the cloth. There is a well-known contemporary account of how the cloth trade was conducted along these lines in the growing town of Exeter. The farmer sent his wool to the market, where it was bought by the spinner. Next week the spun yarn was bought in the same market by the weaver. The following week it was bought as woven cloth by the clothier, who subjected it to finishing processes such as fulling and dyeing and sold it in London or abroad.

This clothier was most likely, perhaps, to be a substantial figure, a genuine capitalist employing a number of workers. There were large employers engaged in the cloth industry who either contracted on a piecework basis or employed a number of workers in their own establishment. In the latter case, the workers were likely to be exploited and ill-paid, like John Winchcombe's men who made their master a fortune, but the most typical "capitalist" of the time was probably the small man, perhaps with no employees other than an apprentice or two, who borrowed capital when he needed it and worked for profit, not wages. He was especially characteristic of the north of England, large employers being found mainly in the south.

Capitalist enterprise was no less evident in the mining industry, where the necessary initial outlay was usually larger. Joint-stock companies were in existence at the time of Shakespeare's birth for the exploitation of mineral resources, predating those organized for trading voyages with which the origin of this type of enterprise is usually associated. Landowners were eager to profit from the resources of their property, and the gentry and nobility were just as prominent as city men in the expansion of the mining industry.

The amount of coal mined was small because wood was still used in iron-smelting; but this very fact encouraged the industry's growth. A great deal of iron was used, and therefore a great deal of wood was burned. Many people were worried by the country's diminishing timber resources, a particularly sensitive point in England where wood was regarded primarily as a material for building ships, and therefore essential to national defence.

Another cause of the expansion of coal-mining was the growth of towns, where coal was frequently

used in the 16th century as a household fuel. Most of London's supply came from Newcastle—by sea, which explains the frequent references in literature to "sea-coal" which have puzzled so many. Between 1545 and 1625 the trade increased tenfold, achieving for a time a faster rate of increase than at the height of the Industrial Revolution! Ease of transport explained Newcastle's dominance. Indeed, transport problems were the most serious limitations of the industry: England had—and has—vast deposits of coal, and in the 16th century there was plenty of it near enough the surface to be easily mined.

From the reign of Elizabeth, with its influx of craftsmen from the continent, can be dated the rise of many minor industries which, if not unknown in England, were relatively small and primitive. Glass-making is one example. Of course, there was a native glass industry, largely located in Kent and Sussex, which had flourished since Norman times or soon after; with the size of the windows in 15th- and 16th-century buildings there was obviously a healthy demand for the product. Besides window glass, glass drinking vessels of a kind had been made since the 14th century at least, and in the 16th century they displayed considerable expertise, the glass-makers of Sussex being celebrated for their skill in a verse of 1557.

In the reign of Edward VI (1547-53) eight Venetians were brought over by a Flemish businessman, Jean Carré, to start a glassworks in London, but they did not stay long; the effort to create a rival to Murano failed. However, the Venetians were only the first of many foreign craftsmen, mainly from France, to bring more modern ideas to the English glass industry. Stourbridge and Newcastle, close to coal supplies and therefore not dependent on wood, became centres of the industry and, although the metal remained greenish, fragments of glass vessels in the looped style of Venice remain as evidence of the pretensions of the new glassmakers. About 1570 Carré set up another glassworks in London, again staffed by Italians, and he seems to have been responsible for the first use in England of imported *barilla* from Spain, which greatly improved the material. When he died in 1572, the works were taken over by one of the Venetians, Jacopo Verzelini who, when the works were burned down, opened another factory and applied for a patent for "the making of drinking glasses such as be accustomably made in the town of Murano"—but cheaper. One or two surviving drinking glasses of the 1580s are ascribed to Verzelini. After his death in 1606, Verzelini's monopoly was held for half a century by a man named Mansell, who was the first to make looking glasses in large numbers. Compelled to use coal, when timber was forbidden altogether for glass furnaces, Mansell was the originator of that English special-

ity, flint glass (modern English "flint glass", however, contains no flint).

INNS AND TAVERNS

Inns provided lodging as well as food and drink; taverns provided refreshment only, not beds. They were extremely popular and were very numerous, although it is impossible to say how many there were. One list dating from the 1570s puts the total number of drinking houses in England at over 16,000, but it clearly did not include every little pot-house between Falmouth and Berwick. Many taverns in the towns had once been simply cook-shops, and they were not structurally different from an ordinary house. A tavern could be recognised by its red-painted lattice, or by ivy or holly hanging up outside. It also had a sign, as taverns still do, but in the 16th century tradesmen's shops and merchants' houses also often had distinguishing signs, so this was not a sure way to recognize a tavern. However, signs of a particularly splendid

Left, the magnificent façade of an inn, at Ludlow, in the Midlands. Above, a pub with a 13th-century façade.

sort—costing, we are told, up to £40 each—were becoming associated with inns and taverns. Inns also had pictures on the walls inside, still a comparatively novel form of decoration. Shakespeare's Sir John Falstaff thought them preferable to tattered and dirty old tapestries.

Their great number, and the numerous references to them in the plays of the period, are evidence of the popularity of inns. There, according to Parson Harrison, the Englishman could behave exactly as if he were in his own home. Foreign travellers were impressed by English inns (more than they are now), and surviving inventories suggest that inns were better equipped with linen and furnishings than one might suspect, although the patriotic Harrison surely exaggerates when he assures his readers that they can be certain of freshly laundered sheets, or that some inns could hold 300 people.

Yet inns did often cater for the great—not all the "rooms where Queen Elizabeth slept" in English hotels are frauds—and some of them may well have been as sumptuous as Harrison says. They were often better in provincial towns than in London, because four or five inns in a small space in competition with each other bred greater keenness than the sprawling capital encouraged.

Harrison apart, inns had plenty of critics. In particular, the inn servant seems to have had a bad reputation. His dilatory performance of his service is guyed bu Shakespeare in *Henry IV* Part II but worse than the poor service was his alleged dishonesty. As it was considered "bad form" for a gentleman to give too much attention to his bill, it was not difficult to overcharge him. Moreover, inn servants where widely believed to be in cahoots with local highwaymen, advising them of travellers likely to prove worth robbing.

Some of Shakespeare's most humorous scenes of comedy are set in The Boar's Head, Eastcheap, making it the most famous of London taverns.

It existed as a tavern as early as the 1530s and perhaps much earlier, though it did not long outlast Shakespeare. Another popular establishment was the Dagger Inn, Holborn, a rather rough place but famous for its powerful ale (most landlords in the 16th century brewed their own) and for its meat pies, which were ornamented with a dagger having a magpie impaled thereon (whether this bird had any significance regarding the contents of the pie it would be hard to say). Ben Jonson seems to have been a customer at the Dagger, which is mentioned in more than one of his plays.

Two famous rivals in Cheapside were the Mitre and the Mermaid, both of which also crop up in contemporary literature. But confusion sometimes arises because there was more than one tavern in London with the same name. There were at least two well-known taverns called the Mitre. The one where Ben Jonson and William Shakespeare used to conduct their verbal duels—Jonson, like a Spanish galleon, the more substantial and soundly based, Shakespeare the nimbler vessel, outmaneuvring him as the English ships did the Armada—was in Holborn. According to a verse by Thomas Heywood which describes the different types of client attracted by the various London taverns, the Mitre was the resort of churchmen, but that was probably the Mitre off Cheapside. Neither of them can be identified with the place where Samuel Johnson used to hold court in the 18th century.

The gatherings of literary men in the London taverns, with wit and wisdom flowing as freely as the wine, are not merely the romantic imaginings of posterity. Francis Beaumont, best-known for his playwright's partnership with Fletcher, remembered them in his *Epistle to Ben Jonson*, writing of the club founded by Raleigh, and attended by Shakespeare among others, which met at the Mermaid: "What things have we seen done at the Mermaid!"

GLOBE. SOUTHWARKE.

10. ENTERTAINMENT

THE THEATRE

The first, specially built, permanent theatre in England was constructed in 1576 by James Burbage, father of Richard, the actor who was Shakespeare's colleague. He had a royal licence which entitled a group of the Earl of Leicester's men, himself included, to put on public performances of plays in the city of London, under supervision of the Master of the Revels (a court official) and providing that there were no performances during times of prayer or when plagues was rampant (in the 1590s plague kept all the London theatres closed for up to eighteen months at a time). When this licence was granted, it was assumed that the performances would take place in one or other of the large inns in London where it was customary to erect a temporary stage in the inn yard.

Although the city government at this time was not quite so powerful and independent a body as it had once been, it was still able to challenge the right of any authority other than itself to license public performances in the city. And it was not keen on these inn-yard performances. They had often been occasions for riot, disorder and crime, not to mention the injury and aggravation caused when the stage or some other temporary structure connected with it collapsed and injured the spectators. To avoid the restrictions of the city authorities, the early builders erected their theatres outside the city limits.

Theatres were not built because inns were structurally unsatisfactory, and the inn-yards were still used by various companies of actors long after London had acquired many regular theatres. The basic shape was little altered except that theatres were round whereas inn-yards were rectangular or square. But this was no innovation either and might even have been regarded as a drawback. The round shape was copied from bearbaiting pits already in existence, and was intended to create an arena rather than an auditorium, so that other entertainments might also take place.

But inns did have certain disadvantages: they had functions to fulfil which had nothing to do with

Left, a fine reconstruction of the Globe Theatre. Below, play-acting on the village green.

the players. Not all guests were eager for actors to take over the central yard and its surrounding galleries. Moreover, rent had to be paid to the landlord of the inn.

Burbage's theatre was, then, a more versatile building. The stage was moveable; it was supported on trestles or barrels, projecting from the tire house behind, which contained dressing rooms, into the audience. Spectators surrounded the stage on three sides (possibly four, as happened in inn-yards where a gallery above the stage was used by spectators). The audience in the "pit", the circular ground space below the tiers of galleries, stood or sat on benches. There was no roof above their heads, and there was no artificial lighting. Nevertheless, it was an elaborate structure, costing £700 to build.

This first London theatre, which was to the north-east of the city, stood until 1598, when it was pulled down and its timbers used in building the more famous Globe.

Meanwhile, one or two "private" theatres had opened in London. They were designated "private", like certain film theatres of our own day, simply to escape the city regulations and the attacks of the theatre's many critics. They were in ordinary buildings, under cover, and apparently required artificial light. Audiences were smaller, admission prices higher, and the actors were usually boys—cheaper than professional actors.

The first theatre on the south bank of the Thames was the Rose, which opened in 1587 and mounted the performance of part of Shakespeare's first (or second) play, the three-part historical drama of

At Stratford, a copy of the first printed edition of Shakespeare's works. Right, fancy-dress party at an inn.

Henry IV. The Swan, built in 1594, if of special interest because it is the only one of these early theatres of which a contemporary interior view exists—a sketch by an enthusiastic Dutch visitor who, unfortunately, may not have been a very accurate observer. He described the theatre as built of stone or concrete, though it must surely have been, like all the others, of wood. Argument rages long over the precise form of the Elizabethan theatre; we shall never know how it looked down to the last detail.

ACTORS AND ENTERTAINERS

Authority looked on actors, conjurors, jugglers, sellers of ballads, Welsh bards, and other wandering entertainers with an unfavourable eye. Apart from the desire to keep the population immobile (of which the Poor Law was an expression) and the fear of those with even slightly irregular means of support, this attitude was not entirely unreasonable. In a comedy by Middleton, a band of strolling players turns out to be a band of well-organized thieves, and the "sturdy beggars" or vagabonds of the time no doubt included many entertainers of these traditional sorts. Respectability could only be gained through the patronage of some wealthy and well-born man or through a licence from the magistrates.

The first licensed company of travelling actors under the protection of a great patron was the

Earl of Leicester's Men. By the time that Shakespeare joined them—his ambition fired, it is said, by the visit of a company of actors to his native town—they were called the Lord Chamberlain's Men, and in the reign of James I they became the King's Men. A number of other companies were formed in the 1580s and 1590s, and there were two companies of boys—not much loved by professional actors. Boys were also in demand to play women's parts, and they must have been good. An English traveller in Italy was surprised to see women acting as well as boys, and one notable boy actor who died at 13 was the object of an encomium by Ben Jonson for his skill in portraying old men.

Shakespeare's thoughts on acting are naturally of special interest. He is said to have been a good actor himself, though not in the class of Richard Burbage, who was the first to play the great Shakespearean tragic heroes. Assuming that Hamlet represents his author's views correctly, Shakespeare disliked over-acting—what we should call "ham". It is often said that the contemporary style of acting was unnaturally histrionic and declamatory by modern standards, although if that is the case it is difficult to see how a Shakespeare play, which today takes over three hours, could have been despatched in two.

Shakespeare seems to have had a low opinion of acting as a profession. For every favourable reference, there are many more unfavourable. The Sonnets contain many examples. But they were written comparatively early, when old attitudes, typified by the authorities' view of actors as potential vagabonds, were more prevalent. It was absurd to put in this class prosperous gentlemen like Edward Alleyn, founder of Dulwich College (which holds so many reminders of the Shakespearean theatre in its gallery), or Richard Burbage, or indeed Shakespeare himself.

Acting pure and simple was precarious. But established actors usually held a share in the theatre or in the profits from provincial tours. Thus Shakespeare held shares in the Globe theatre, where he had once played the Ghost to Burbage's Hamlet, and he still held them when he died. But the theatre generally had many enemies. Though popular at court, it was regarded as a sink of evil by Puritans, whose views were beginning to have some effect in the city government and in parliament. Only one generation after Shakespeare's death, these views were to become dominant.

Musical scenes: on the left, the musical accompaniment to a banquet given by Sir Henry Unton. Bottom left, a spinet, or virginal, of distinctly English design, which once belonged to Queen Elizabeth I.

MUSIC

English music had been in the European vanguard in the 15th century, but the civil wars which reduced noble patronage and, still more, the Protestant Reformation under Henry VIII were severe setbacks. The Reformation ensured that there would be no English Palestrina.

Yet William Byrd, the greatest English composer of the 16th century, did not fall far short of Palestrina's exalted standard and, in spite of the Reformation, music was the most brilliant feature of the English Renaissance after literature. It may be no coincidence that Byrd, like his mentor Thomas Tallis, was a Roman Catholic (fortunately, that did not prevent him being appointed organist of the Chapel Royal in 1569). Some of the finest music of both composers—and in his four *Masses* Byrd stands level with Palestrina—could only have been heard in private.

Nevertheless, English church music, certainly until the appearance of Orlando Gibbons in the reign of James I, was on the whole less distinguished than secular music. The Puritans would have liked to do away altogether with most church music, certainly anything ornate or elaborate, but the Queen herself let it be known that choirs were expected to go on singing anthems. (She was adept at such informal regulation of these matters: at the start of her reign, when Mary's priests met her outside the church door bearing "papist" tapers, she brusquely ordered them away with the remark that she "could see well enough".)

So the beautiful old churches still echoed with the sound of anthems—too much anthem-singing, said Falstaff, had caused his hoarseness of voice, not too much drink—but religious music remained simpler than in Roman Catholic countries. And the Reformation brought some musical gains. Metrical psalm-singing became very popular with ordinary people through the influence of Protestant refugees from Flanders.

In music as in so many other matters, England was powerfully influenced by Italy. The madrigal, a song in three or four part harmony, unaccompanied, which seems quintessentially English (indeed, quintessentially Elizabethan, for its history was as short as it was brilliant), was an Italian import. John Dowland, along with Morley, Wilbye and others, wrote many madrigals, but he also excelled as a composer of solo songs accompanied

on the lute, in which the traditions of the old troubadours and the balladeers mingled with contemporary Italian influences.

Queen Elizabeth loved music and dancing, and so did her subjects. Folk-dancing was a feature of every local festival and pageant, as well as of the court *masque*. Kempe, a famous comic actor, once did a morris dance from London to Norwich (over 100 miles) to win a bet. In the new theatres being built in Southwark the musicians were hardly less important than the actors, and the frequency of references to music in Shakespeare is well known. (Before the days of computers, indefatigable scholars went through the plays counting each appearance of words like "music", "song", etc. and produced impressive totals: 247 appearances of the verb "sing", for example.)

Nearly everyone seems to have been able to play a musical instrument. The Queen was an expert performer on the virginals, a simple keyboard instrument, and the lute, a stringed instrument plucked with the fingers. When Drake sailed off in the *Golden Hind* to carry the English flag around the world, the ship's company included a small chamber orchestra. Similarly, every large town had its town band, every great household had its musicians, and every great house its "minstrel gallery".

More than forty collections of madrigals were published between 1590 and 1620, and every gentleman's household contained one or two of them. Singing was as popular as playing an instrument, and ballad sheets could be bought from pedlars in the streets. Someone at a house party who confessed that he was unable to sing a part provoked blank astonishment, while if the author of *Praise of Music* (1588) is to be believed, ordinary workers and craftsmen "keep such a chanting and singing in their shops" that the streets resounded with cheerful song.

Facing, an allegory from the Shepherd's Calendar. *As the queen of the shepherds, Queen Elizabeth is honoured in the midst of a chorus of Graces. Right, the Queen dancing; her partner does not hesitate to sweep her off her feet!*

Below, music composed for the nocturnal revelries of the owner of a country house in Essex.

In Elizabethan times, hunting was almost as important at it had been in the Middle Ages. Falconry also continued to be practised. Among the books published on the subject, the principal one is entitled: "The noble Arte of Venerie".

HUNTING AND HAWKING

There is a likely story that Shakespeare as a youth was caught poaching in a nearby forest, a crime very common in England. He certainly knew more about hunting than any writer in England until the 18th century, though he was perhaps more expert in the ways of shooting with the crossbow than hunting with hounds. Deer were hunted for meat as well as sport, and it was not, on the whole, a sportsmanlike business. The deer were often driven into a kind of enclosure where they could be shot in comfort by the assembled company. When we hear of an elderly lady like Queen Elizabeth going hunting, we need not assume any remarkable display of energy. At Cowdray in 1591 the Queen shot four deer from a bower in the park while her musicians played a pleasant air. Although we hear of horses being worn out, English hunting was more of a leisurely amble through the woods, indeed, through the park, until the more advanced hunting techniques of France were introduced in the 17th century.

THE NOBLE ARTE OF
VENERIE OR HVNTING.

VVherein is handled and set out ... vertues, Nature, and Properties of fiuetene sundrie Chaces togither, with the order and maner how to Hunte and kill euery one of them.

Tranſlated and collected for the pleaſure of all Noblemen and Gentlemen, out of the beſt approued Authors, which haue written any thing concerning the ſame: And reduced into ſuch order and proper termes as are vſed here, in this noble Realme of England.

Like hunting, fishing was also popular, but over a much vaster portion of society.

Hounds were slow and ill-trained by later standards. Nevertheless, they were cherished for particular qualities, as we see from the exchange between the lord and his huntsman in the opening scene of *The Taming of the Shrew*, in which the two men argue about the merits of individual hounds. Incidentally, several of the names of the hounds mentioned—Bellman, Merriman—would still be found among modern packs.

By 1600, deer were already becoming less common. The destruction of woodland and the improvement of firearms meant that in the 17th century they would become scarce (Charles II imported deer for the royal parks from Germany), but in Elizabeth's day for one they remained the chief quarry of the hunt. But, as Shakespeare asserted, for good sport the best quarry was the hare, "the most marvellous beast that is", according to a contemporary book on game. There is a long celebration of the hare as the hunter's quarry in Shakespeare's *Venus and Adonis*. The fox, on the other hand, was regarded as no more than

The Booke of Faulconrie or Hauking, FOR THE ONELY DElight and pleasure of all Noblemen and Gentlemen:

Collected out of the best aucthors, asvvell Italians as Frenchmen, and some English practises withall concernyng Faulconrie, the contentes whereof are to be seene in the next page folowyng.

By *George Turberuile* Gentleman.

NOCET EMPTA DOLORE VOLVPTAS.

vermin. Although it was occasionally hunted by gentlemen with hounds, it was treated as a most inferior animal whose disposal should best be left to humbler folk. The Elizabethans would have been astonished to learn what prestige fox-hunting was to acquire in England two hundred years later.

Hawking seems to have been popular with most classes of the population; Shakespeare clearly expected his audience to be familiar with the technical terms of falconry. *A Treatise of Hawks and Hawking*, published in 1619, was almost the only original English book (there were a number copied from French works) on any aspect of field sports. The most "sporting" bird was the peregrine falcon, a high flyer relatively common in northern Europe until recently, but the short-winged sparrow-hawk and goshawk were no less effective if the prime aim was to fill the pot. The merlin, a smaller falcon, was especially popular with ladies.

Other popular field sports of the time included coursing, chasing the hare with greyhounds; fowling, shooting birds or catching them in traps; and fishing with rod and line.

A book on falconry, by George Turberville, Gentleman, *appeared in 1575. Dogs were still used for hunting, and were cared for with all due attention.*

The English have always been a nation of pet-lovers. The print on the right-hand page shows a vet treating a dog.

ANIMAL-BAITING

The age of Elizabeth is full of ironies, and none greater than the situation in close proximity on the south bank of the Thames at London of two nearly identical buildings. One of them was the Globe Theatre, where the greatest plays ever written were receiving their first performances. The other was the Bearpit, where helpless animals were torn by dogs for the amusement of the spectators. To further the irony, it is clear that people drew little distinction between the different entertainments provided in the two buildings. Edward Alleyn and his father-in-law, Philip Henslowe, who were the greatest impresarios of the age, divided their time equally between managing theatre plays and bear-baitings; Henslowe eventually built a new building which could be used for both.

Bear baiting and bullbaiting were very old sports (if that is the word), never more popular than in 16th-century England. They were conducted in private parks and public squares all over the country, though the establishments at Southwark (including the arena for bullbaiting), with a capacity for 1,000 spectators, were the chief centres.

The bear was attached to a post by a chain, and half a dozen mastiffs were set upon him. After he had killed or badly mauled one or two, the rest would become less bold, and though new dogs were introduced, the affair might become a stand-off. It seems that the bear was seldom fatally hurt; his keeper would tend his wounds so that he might fight another day. Bears, after all, had to be imported and were therefore valuable. Bulls were allowed to run free, pursued by dogs and, sometimes, men on horseback. Other animals, such as boars, were also baited, and a popular concluding act was to set dogs after a monkey mounted on a horse. King James, in an effort to raise the status of the sport, arranged for the baiting of lions in the Tower of London.

"What Christian heart", inquired Philip Stubbes, "can take pleasure to see one poor beast rend, tear and kill another...?" The answer was practically everyone, from the Queen downward. And this in spite of the notorious rowdiness of the spectators, which caused great annoyance to those living nearby, and of the danger of serious accident when the bear broke free from its chain, as seems to have happened quite often. The government resisted attempts to have bear gardens closed down, an interesting contrast with its attitude towards other rowdy entertainments, such as football. In Southwark, the crowds were safely confined in one restricted space and could be allowed to work off their aggression unmolested. Football, unrestricted in area, seemed much more dangerous.

According to persistent rumours, cock-fighting still goes on secretly in remote parts of England. In the 16th century few people thought it particularly cruel, and the first cockpit specially built was ordered by King Henry VIII. There is a curiously shaped public house in St Albans (near the ruins of the Roman town) which was once used as a cockpit, and in Elizabeth's reign there were many cockpits in London. A famous passage in *Henry IV* describes the theatre as a cockpit.

On a visit to Lincoln in 1617 King James I ordered a cock fight to be held for his amusement at an inn. Four cocks were put into the ring together, which gave His Majesty extra amusement. The cocks, the fiercest being bred in Norfolk, at this period fought with natural equipment only. It was not until later in the century that metal spurs were added.

In this amusing print (opposite) a football is being inflated. Above, tennis being played, on a covered court.

SPORTS AND GAMES

Sports and games in Elizabethan England could be divided into two classes: those of which Authority approved, and those of which it did not —including some that were banned by law. Alternatively, they could be divided into the two classes described by Roger Ascham as "containing either some fit exercise for war, or some pleasant pastime for peace". Oddly enough, it was the former group that tended to find favour with Authority. There was a feeling that exercise ought to be designed for some purpose, specifically for expertise in battle, and also that games in which a large number were involved were all too likely to end in riot.

The government was especially worried by the decline of archery. The longbow was the fundamental infantry weapon, which had proved its worth in the 100 Year's War. Virtually every able-bodied man was expected to be able to use one. Shakespeare, as usual, shows himself to be fully conversant with the most technical aspects of archery, and he clearly assumed that his audience would be able to follow him. Yet archery was in something of a crisis in the 16th century. A number of laws were passed to promote it and several contemporary authors warn of impending doom as a result of the neglect of archery, which seems to have been the result of the increasing use of guns (though by 1600 the gun had not yet proved beyond doubt its superiority to the bow and arrow: Leicester took many bowmen to the Netherlands in 1585), and, in sport, the growing popularity of the cross-bow—a weapon which, it has been said, demands less practice.

If archery was declining, fencing was rising, thanks largely to the introduction of the rapier from Italy. The old English fight of sword and buckler, or shield, was already old-fashioned in Elizabethan times: Hotspur, in *Henry IV* Part II jeers at "that sword-and-buckler Prince of Wales".

Fencing might be called a "court" sport. In the country, less elegant contests were practised. Wrestling, however, was common at all levels of society—Henry VIII had wrestled with François I at their famous meeting on the Field of the Cloth of Gold—but it was often very dangerous to limb and, indeed, to life. There is some question during the wrestling scene in *As You Like It* as to whether it was a fit sight for ladies.

A vast number of games, some of then com-

pletely mysterious and known only by enigmatic names, were played by Shakespeare's contemporaries. Ball games are of special interest to us, although examination of the ball games played in 16th-century England casts grave doubts on that well-known English assumption that virtually all ball games were invented in England. On the contrary, a sophisticated form of football, with forwards, half-backs and full backs, was being played in Florence in the 16th century when football in England could still be justly described as "nothing but beastly fury and extreme violence". It had advanced little from the legendary first game of Anglo-Saxon football in which the ball was the head of a Viking. However, all attempts to strangle the game out of existence failed, and in the reign of James I the authorities gave up the struggle. There were even some gestures towards encouraging it, and the Puritans had no special objection to football unless, of course, it was played on Sundays.

The family of games of which the most popular modern examples are tennis and squash appear to have originated not in England but in France, where the early *jeu de paume* may have been similar to the modern English game of fives, or handball. The English word "tennis" probably comes from the French *tenez*. The tennis of the 16th century was of course the game now known as "real" or "royal" tennis, played in a court equipped with apparently arbitrary hazards which betray the origins of the game in a monastic courtyard. The tennis court of Henry VIII at Hampton Court is still in use today, although it has been rebuilt more than once since the 16th century. One of Shakespeare's most memorable sporting metaphors embraces all the major technical terms of tennis.

While staying with the Earl of Hertford, Queen Elizabeth once watched a game played below her chamber window on "a square green court", marked with lines, by ten of the Earl's servants—five a side. Some have seen in this an early form of lawn tennis; but all attempts to establish genealogies for modern games founder on the complete absence of central administration before the 19th century, which makes it almost pointless to talk about "tennis", "football" or any other game as early as the 16th century.

Even cricket, indubitably an English game (though there is a not totally implausible French claim to have invented cricket too), can barely

be discerned in Shakespeare's England. There is a reference to schoolboys at Guildford playing cricket in 1550, but the first full description of what is recognisably the ancestor of the modern game dates from over 100 years later.

The ball game mentioned most frequently in Shakespeare is bowls, in which a ball with a built-in bias is rolled along the ground towards a target. It was this game, according to one of the most cherished of patriotic legends, that Drake was playing at Plymouth when the Armada was first sighted. On being told of its approach, Drake's alleged response was that there was time to finish the game and then beat the Spaniards. Bowls had its critics too. "A bowl-alley", said John Earle, "is the place where there are three things thrown away besides bowls, to wit, time and money".

There were a great many similar games, including games of skittles similar to the games still played in bar parlours in rural districts. Golf was well-established in Scotland: one of the misdeeds ascribed to Mary Queen of Scots was that she had gone out to play golf a few days after her husband's murder, and when James VI became James I of England in 1603, his luggage on the journey south included a set of golf-clubs.

The picture reproduced above has the title "gentle-men playing Primero". Right, the children of the Earl of Windsor prefer chess.

INDOOR GAMES

The English have always been a race of addicted gamblers, and many games existed simply to gratify this addiction, which helps to explain why some apparently harmless games, such as skittles, were banned. The most common form of gambling, probably, was with dice, and men spoke of dicing in much the same way as they spoke of drinking or wenching—as a mild, enjoyable, and practically universal vice. The very word "hazard" was originally, it appears, the name of a certain dice game.

Gambling encourages the urge to cheat, and cheating at dice was not difficult for the crafty. Making false dice was a favourite occupation in London prisons. At cards, cheating was still easier: we hear of marked cards, bent corners, and a hundred other deceits, which must have been all the more easily practised when playing cards were manufactured with less precision than they are now. Puritans naturally objected to gambling and they had a particular objection to cards: they suspected that the picture cards had first arisen as "images

If on your man you light
The first draught shall you play,
If not t:s mine by right
At first to lead the way

This amusing print (bottom left) bears a very wise maxim.
Bottom right, a playing card from the Elizabethan period.

of idols and false gods".

A favourite card game among the upper classes was primero, Spanish in origin which, like most gambling games, appears to have been fairly simple, although we do not know exactly how it was played. On a more intellectual level, chess was a popular pastime. The young Elizabeth used to play it with her tutor, although James I, surprisingly, did not care for it. It seems to have been something of a ladies' game, perhaps because women's intellectual ability had few other outlets: Saul's *The Famous Game of Chess-Play,* published in 1614, was dedicated to the Countess of Bedford. Shakespeare we may guess, was not a chess-player, for he scarcely mentions the game in spite of the abundant scope it offers for puns, something that his fellow-playwrights frequently exploited.

Besides draughts, the handmaiden of chess, a very popular table game was backgammon, which has suddenly returned to favour in the 1970s. There were also several games bearing a relationship to the modern "pub" game of "shove ha'—penny"—in which coins are slid along a smooth, polished board.

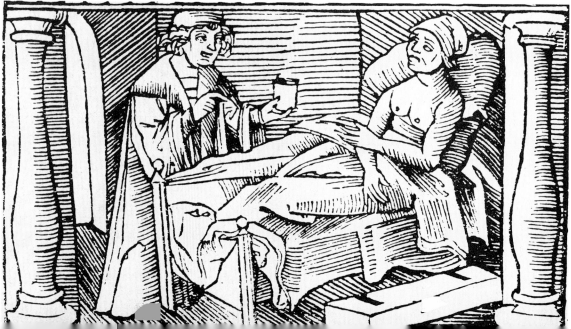

13. SCIENCE AND MEDICINE

THE ADVANCE OF SCIENCE

The "scientific revolution" is usually regarded as belonging to the late 17th century—the age of Newton. But, like most other intellectual "*revolutions*", its beginnings can be discerned much earlier, certainly in the reign of Elizabeth I. The science of the 16th century was once thought to be almost wholly worthless—a dismal landscape of superstition, ancient prejudice and deliberate fraud marked only by the occasional peak represented by a man like Bacon, with his belief in the experimental method. But recent research has shown that there was more to Elizabethan science than that.

One can also detect signposts pointing more or less directly towards the Industrial Revolution of the late 18th century (in the century after the accession of Elizabeth, coal-mining increased at a greater rate than it did in the century after 1775). There were advances in mining and smelting methods and fast-growing knowledge of metallurgy, though this derived largely from the Germans.

According to Dr A.L. Rowse, one in ten of the books published in the reign of Elizabeth was devoted to some kind of scientific subject. Books on "natural history" were fast replacing the fabulous "bestiaries" of the Middle Ages, and even attempting some rough classification of flora and fauna. The first English *Pharmacopoeia* was published in London in 1618.

Some able men were at work in study and laboratory. John Dee did extraordinary things in many different fields, some in fields, it must be admitted, not worth tilling. Thomas Harriot was a brilliant mathematician who advanced some way towards analytical geometry, while John Napier of Merchiston invented logarithms. Much good work was done on navigation, on lenses (it is not certain what exactly were the "perspective glasses" owned by several Elizabethan scientists) and on navigational instruments. The study of botany in England was first placed on a serious basis by William Turner (1510-68). William Gilbert (1540-1603) founded the study of electro-magnetism, while William Harvey (1578-1657) discovered the circulation of the blood.

The office of the doctor (none other than Shakespeare's brother-in-law) who wrote the Treatise whose title-page is reproduced on the right.

Select Observations ON *ENGLISH* BODIES: OR, Cures both Empericall and Historicall, performed upon very eminent Persons in desperate Diseases.

First, written in Latine by Mr. *John Hall* Physician, living at *Stratford* upon *Avon* in *Warrick-shire*, where he was very famous, as also in the Counties adjacent, as appeares by these Observations drawn out of severall hundreds of his, as choysest.

Now put into English for common benefit by *James Cooke* Practitioner in *Physick* and *Chirurgery*.

Below, Elizabethan anaesthetics: the patient was made to inhale alcohol fumes.

A doctor and some of his activities.

PHYSICIANS, SURGEONS AND APOTHECARIES

Shakespeare's plays provide a rich field of examples of the characteristic mixture of sense and superstition that made up medical ideas and practice at the end of the 16th century. One of the most enlightened of Elizabethan commentators on health believed completely in the efficacy of a certain type of precious stone as a preventative against plague, while scornfully attacking the mumbo-jumbo of astrology.

In medicine as in other matters, England was somewhat backward. A work on anatomy published in the 1570s was no more than a copy of a 14th-century manuscript, in spite of the fact that the subject had been revolutionized by the work of the Flemish anatomist, Vesalius, who died in

the eighth year of Elizabeth's reign. Although the College of Physicians was founded, largely through the efforts of Thomas Linacre, as early as 1518, and there were professional chairs of medicine at both Oxford and Cambridge, aspiring English physicians usually went to a foreign school—Padua, where Vesalius had lectured, or Montpellier, Basle, or Heidelberg. This foreign education of doctors was sometimes resented; it was feared that all they were likely to learn in Italy was skill with poisons.

The physician enjoyed high professional status and charged relatively high fees: his services were not for the poor, who had to make do with the spells of the local wise woman or the prescriptions doled out—in spite of the efforts of the College of Physicians to prevent it—by the parish priest. (However, to be deprived of professional medical services was not necessarily a disadvantage). In

130

The surgeon John Banister giving an anatomy lesson.

one Welsh town, a physician was lured into residence by the waiving of the fee normally payable by burgesses and the promise of a regular salary. But this early example of a local officer of health undertook to treat only his fellow-burgesses.

The College of Physicians did try to keep standards high. It did not issue its licences to practice too freely, and insisted on candidates having a university education, though its standards were less rigorous for those practising deep in the country than for physicians in the capital. In 1565 it gained the right to dissect human corpses at its headquarters at Amen Corner (executed criminals were regularly provided) and all fellows were compelled to attend these demonstrations. Vesalian anatomy was also expounded by Dr Caius in Cambridge, at the college which still bears his name, and by the surgeons at Barber's Hall.

The greatest physician of the age was William Harvey (1578-1657), who was educated at Gonville and Caius College and at Padua, where he studied the workings of the valves of the heart. His great discovery was the circulation of the blood, and although, like most great scientific advances, Harvey's discovery was not the isolated flash of brilliance that it appears in brief histories, there is no doubt of the genuineness of his achievement. He did not publish his work until 1628, although he had expounded his ideas in lectures many years earlier. (Physicians, or others, felt no compulsion to publish discoveries for the benefit of mankind or the advance of knowledge: the Chamberlen family kept the invention of obstetric forceps a secret for several years.)

Harvey was a great man in his own time, and he was not alone among physicians to achieve im-

portant social status. Another famous doctor was Sir Theodore de Mayerne, a Huguenot refugee said to have been responsible for introducing the drug calomel. He attended many important patients including the Prince of Wales (son of James I) who unfortunately died young—probably, to judge by Sir Theodore's report of his illness, of typhoid.

There is evidence in Shakespeare's plays that can be interpreted as implying the dramatist's awareness of Harvey's discovery of the circulation of the blood, although that interpretation depends on a rather biased reading and such knowledge on Shakespeare's part seems highly unlikely if not impossible. Like others, Shakespeare did believe wholeheartedly in the medieval notion of the "humours" of the body. This envisaged four basic bodily fluids, or "humours": blood, phlegm, choler (yellow bile) and melancholy (black bile). Their relative proportions governed character: thus a man might be sanguine, phlegmatic, choleric or melancholy in temperament. An excess of one or other of the humours caused disease, it was thought, and the remedy was to reduce it by bleeding or by a purgative. This curious belief took a very long time to die. It far outlasted Harvey's discovery of the circulation of the blood; while the belief in the efficacy of bleeding for various complaints was still current within living memory.

The surgeon has suffered in reputation by his association with the barber, for they shared a common association—the Company of Barber Surgeons. Though the barber's surgery was limited to blood-letting, teeth-pulling and little more, the status of the surgeon was certainly inferior to that of the physician, under whose instructions he often

operated. However, many surgeons were more skilful and more knowledgeable than the common image of the fellow who would let blood or shave a beard equally upon request suggests. William Clowes, for example, who was a surgeon with Leicester's troops in the Netherlands, was an authority on wounds and wrote several books on the subject—and in English, not Latin.

By and large, however, surgeons had a poor reputation, and the reference in *Twelfth Night* to the surgeon who was too drunk to treat his patients would have struck a popular chord.

Apothecaries were no better. They were often regarded as poseurs and cheats. They did not get their own royal charter until 1616, having previously been associated with the Company of Grocers and subject to the control of the Physicians, who had the power to inspect an apothecary's stock. As one contemporary put it, the apothecary was in reality no more than "the Physician's Cook", making up medicines to order.

Not surprisingly, there were large opportunities for "quack" doctors, "folk" remedies and other manifestations of unofficial medicine. The Barber Surgeons were bound by their charter to permit the dispensation of herbs and liquids by persons who, though unqualified, were commonly supposed to have knowledge of such matters, and this clause let in all sorts. A partial check was introduced when the Company took to issuing licences for a short period only, whereafter they were reviewed and, if malpractice were discovered, the holder was expelled.

Superstition and credulity were not confined to the uneducated, and unqualified practitioners of various arts might find patrons at the highest levels of society. The College of Physicians showed some courage and determination in pursuing these well-protected imposters. It restrained from practice one quack who was a personal medical adviser to no less a figure than Sir Francis Walsingham, secretary of state; and it later obtained an apology from Walsingham for his opposition to the College over this case. In another case, the College moved against a herbalist favoured by the Queen. How much this vigilance of the Physicians was due to plain professional rivalry and how much to a genuine desire to safeguard the population from the hazards of unskilled or unqualified doctoring it would be hard to say. No doubt both motives were at work.

PLAGUE

Until the late 17th century, plague, a disease of rats which is transmitted to humans by their fleas, was a regular visitor to England. The great outbreak known as the Black Death, with the recurring waves that followed every ten or twelve years from the mid 14th to the early 15th century, had killed more than one-third of the population. After 1400 the attacks became less severe and less widely pervasive. In the 16th century, plague was restricted to London and, to a lesser extent, large provincial towns.

There were particularly serious attacks of plague in London in the years 1592, 1602 and 1603. It was the custom for theatres to close when the death rate reached thirty a week, and that happened nearly every summer—the season of plague. Those who were able to go normally left the city during the summer months; hence, partly at least, the peregrinations of Queen and court among the country mansions of exalted subjects. "Seeing that we have sent our children forth three weeks past into a good air and a sweet country, let us follow them" says the Citizen's Wife in *A Dialogue Against the Pestilence* (first published in 1564). "Let us take leave of our neighbours, and return... home again when the plague is past, and the dog days ended". (quoted Dover Wilson *op cit* p. 136).

Plague may still be a deadly disease, and the 16th century had no defence against it, except flight. Nevertheless, many specifics were offered against plague and some cures were confidently prescribed. Gervase Markham, in his *English*

Housewife (1516) gave a recipe for creating immunity to plague the basis of which was "a quart of old ale" (a good basis for any cure no doubt), to which were added a number of more or less enigmatic substances including a much-favoured medicine of the time called dragon water. The mixture was to be taken first thing in the morning, and afterwards a piece of dried root of angelica was to be chewed. Although the author insisted that this safeguard was found to be effective, he also prescribed treatment for a patient suffering from plague. Part of it involved the application of "a live pigeon cut in two parts" to the symptomatic swellings of the disease.

Curiously, plague vanished from England as mysteriously as it had arrived. There was a very serious outbreak in London in 1665, but it was the last. In the following summer, the Great Fire destroyed most of medieval London and the city was rebuilt largely in brick and stone, rather than wood and plaster. It seems that at about this time the black rat—the main carrier of plague—was being supplanted by the less deadly (except to black rats) brown rat. Other factors may also have been significant. At any rate, from then onward the fearful horror of plague vanished almost completely.

THE NEW ASTRONOMY AND THE OLD ASTROLOGY

Throughout the Middle Ages, and for the great majority in the 16th century too, Ptolemy's explanation of the universe was accepted without question. According to that ancient scholar, the earth was the centre of the universe; sun, moon, planets and stars revolved around it, each in its particular sphere, and when the spheres rubbed together they produced the music of the spheres, to which there are so many references in contemporary literature. Many intelligent men held this belief; Hooker, for instance, the author of the great philosophical justification of the Church of England, adhered to the Ptolemaic system which, indeed, seemed to be proved by ordinary observation. Like the character in Bernard Shaw's *St. Joan*, any fool could see that the sun moved around the earth, and Elizabethan Englishmen were frequent and accurate observers of the heavenly bodies. They navigated by the stars and, on clear nights, they told the time by the position of heavenly bodies.

In scientific circles, if such a term is not anachronistic, the Ptolemaic system was long out of date. In 1543 Copernicus, a Polish monk, had published his *De revolutionibus orbium coelestium,* which advanced the theory that the sun was the centre of the solar system, and that the planets, including earth, moved around it. The Copernican theory was confirmed beyond reasonable doubt by the work of Kepler and Galileo in the early 17th century, but before that it was widely accepted in Europe—at least among the small minority of informed people. It was not accepted by everyone even within that small minority. Bacon, for example, though he would not swallow the old Ptolemaic explanation, did not believe Copernicus either and invented his own, somewhat bizarre, explanation of the universe. But men like the mathematician Harriot, who was a friend of Kepler, and that ubiquitous scholar Dr John Dee, were convinced Copernicans. Nor were the English backward in every respect compared with their European counterparts. Men like Harriot owned a "perspective glass", which seems to have been a primitive kind of telescope, before the generally accepted date of the invention of that instrument.

England's most important contribution to this

early stage in the revolution of physical sciences, which was to culminate in Newton's discovery of the law of gravity about a century later, was the work of William Gilbert, physician to the Queen, who in his book on magnetism published in 1600 announced the important discovery that the earth is a great magnet. Though less well known than Bacon or Dee or even Harriot, Gilbert was the greatest English scientist of the age and his *De Magnete* one of the most influential works of the century. Galileo knew and admired his work, though Bacon discounted him in spite of the fact that Gilbert was a prime exponent of the "scientific method", as advocated by Bacon.

It was widely believed that goings-on in the heavens had important—and usually dire—effects on earth. Comets, for example, were particularly ominous and, as several references in Shakespeare make plain, were associated with the death of great rulers. Eclipses were, understandably, also fearful, as the author of *A Wonderful Astrological Prognostication* (1591) mockingly demonstrated: "It is further to be feared that because the eclipse happeneth in July, there will through the extreme heat grow such abundance of fleas that women shall not go to bed before twelve o'clock at night, for the great murders and stratagems they are likely to commit upon those little animals". (Quoted Dover Wilson, *op cit* page 46).

Astrology was an applied science compared with the "pure" science of astronomy, and someone like Dr Dee could believe in Copernican astronomy while practising assiduously as an astrologer—though it is hard to be sure to what extent men of his kind really believed their own mumbo-jumbo. Some men said, with Kepler, that astrology was "the foolish daughter of a wise mother". Others were less tolerant.

As we see today, any method of allegedly foretelling the future is ensured of some popularity, and astrology survived the strictures of reformers such as Calvin just as it had survived the condemnation of Rome two centuries earlier. It was also a great comfort to many people to believe that their misfortunes, or their vices, were inevitable, ordained by the stars, that they were "villains by necessity", as Shakespeare puts it in *King Lear*.

In Elizabethan England the stars were still examined more often for astrological purposes than for any other—as, indeed, to judge from the popular press, they are to this day. Yet astrology was already sinking out of favour. It was so full of absurdities that educated people found it increasingly hard to swallow, and it was fast becoming part of that great mass of fraud, trickery and false pretences which, like weeds around a pond, formed such a large fringe of society.

12. RELIGIOUS BELIEF

THE CHURCH OF ENGLAND

The Elizabethan Church Settlement of 1559 caused great argument then and has done so ever since. How much did it represent a general consensus? According to the Spanish ambassador, two-thirds of the country was Roman Catholic, and other Catholics put the number even higher. Protestants naturally scoff at such estimates. But the truth probably is that for the great mass of the population, the religious settlement was not a matter of great moment at all. Not that they were unreligious. It was simply that this was the fourth religious settlement within the lifetime of comparatively young people. Moreover, few people were concerned with—or understood—questions of Church constitution or religious doctrine.

Nor, of course, were the people consulted, except insofar as parliament represented their opinions (another very questionable matter). The clergy were not asked either. The Elizabethan settlement was predominantly a political settlement (the Church of England had no established body of doctrine until the publication of the 39 Articles in 1563), and it was imposed from above, though enshrined in the parliamentary acts of supremacy and uniformity. Failure to adhere to these acts carried severe penalties: a word in favour of the Pope could be construed as treason; failure to attend church cost 12 pence a time; clergymen who refused to take the oath of supremacy, acknowledging the Queen as "supreme governor" of the Church, lost their livings.

The settlement was not so rigid as it looked, partly because it was not rigidly enforced. In certain respects there was an obvious attempt to avoid controversy; for example, the prayer to be delivered from the tyranny of the "bishop of Rome" in the Second Prayer Book of Edward VI. which formed the basis for the Elizabethan Prayer Book, was omitted. To the ordinary subject, indeed, the obvious, radical differences between the Protestant Church of England and the Church of Rome were relatively few.

The anti-Catholic disturbances, including a new outbreak of image-breaking, which were the inevitable result of the ascendancy of Protestantism after the reaction of Mary's reign, were sharply suppressed. Although most of the bishops refused to accept the act of supremacy or the new Prayer Book and accordingly lost their livings, only a few

were imprisoned (and not for long), while the lower clergy overwhelmingly accepted the settlement. This did not mean that they were all convinced Protestants, merely that only a few of them were so passionately attached to the Church of Rome that they were prepared to lose their livings and perhaps go into exile, or exist in secret, for its sake.

The general acceptance by the parish clergy meant that the great majority of the lay population also accepted the Elizabethan Church settlement. There were, naturally, exceptions, especially in the North of England, which remained almost solidly Catholic and filled the new, northern bishops with despair. Otherwise, many English Catholics managed to compromise in some way. Some might go to Church of England services in public, and to Roman Catholic services in private—and such was the confusion of the times that there were places where the same clergyman officiated at both services!

Left, a sermon in the courtyard of St. Paul's Cathedral. Below, title page from a contemporary edition of the Bible.

The Church was still part of government. Elizabeth ruled through the bishops just as, in secular affairs, she ruled through royal councillors and magistrates. The virtues of her bishops—sound administration, honour combined with practical flexibility, religious zeal in moderation—were very much the virtues of her magistrates. Elizabeth's government was, on the whole, wisely inclined to let sleeping dogs lie—not to make windows into men's souls, as the Queen put it. Although there was some tightening up of the laws against nonconformity in 1563, by 16th-century standards the government was tolerant. This was made possible by the policy of Philip II, the major defender of the old order in Europe, who held back the more aggressive schemes of the Pope. This situation was changed drastically after the Pope's excommunication of Elizabeth in 1670, but even then many Catholics survived more or less openly and some held official positions.

As an organ of government, the Church still had its courts, which in the Middle Ages had formed a dual system with the royal courts. They had lost some of their jurisdiction and were in accelerating decline, but there were other ecclesiastical courts, such as the Court of High Commission, which had developed out of an investigatory commission appointed in the reign of Henry VIII. This court became the chief weapon of Whitgift, appointed archbishop of Canterbury in 1583, in his battle with the Puritans. The battle, again, was almost totally political: it was concerned with the government of the Church, not its doctrine or even its ritual. The Court of High Commission, with bishops and church lawyers as its judges, acquired considerable influence in the 1580s and was used by Whitgift to enforce his edicts against the Puritans. It was much resented even in high quarters: Burghley made a famous protest in which he compared the court's operations to those of the Inquisition. Parliament also complained, but Whitgift had the support of the Queen, who was no less determined than he that the Church of England should not be subverted from within.

SUPERSTITION AND WITCHCRAFT

The atmosphere of *Midsummer Night's Dream* or *The Tempest* would possibly have seemed less alien to the people for whom the plays were written

140

Left, a Bible-reading in St. Paul's. Below, witches: superstition was particularly widespread in the country areas.

than it does to us. Contemporaries would have found the apparitions seen by Marlowe's Faustus or Shakespeare's Macbeth less improbable. For ordinary people were still surrounded by a web of medieval superstition. They were familiar with the idea of fairies, goblins, ghosts (rather frequent in Shakespeare), devils, spirits and a host of other supernatural beings. Many people would not walk past a graveyard at night, would not complete a journey if a hare ran across their path, smashed empty eggshells after eating the egg so that witches, could not use them for boats, made their will if they heard a raven croaking in the night. Magic charms, spells and amulets—"tricks... to cheat the devil", as Shakespeare put it—were in great demand to safeguard against sickness or ward off evil influences. One cure for a headache was to tie around one's head the rope which had been used to hang a criminal—something not too difficult to come by in those times. A quite depressingly large number of incidents, objects and animals were in some way "unlucky"; far fewer were lucky. Any kind of unusual or unnatural behaviour was ascribed to spells or enchantments or, in the case, for example, of some disfiguring human malformation, the punishment of God. The old Church had encouraged many superstitions, and the new religion made little progress against them.

Divination was sometimes practised, though by less grisly means than "reading" the entrails of a fowl—that favourite Roman method. One common way was to open the Bible at random; it was certain to fall open at some verse which appeared to be significant. In most villages there were one or two elderly women with a reputation for making predictions and it was commonly believed that the dying were capable of prophecy: hence the famous dying speech of John of Gaunt in Shakespeare's *Richard II* ("Methinks I am a prophet new inspired..."). Dreams also were regarded with superstitious respect. It was believed that dreams dreamed in the morning would come true.

Most scholarly men were regarded as likely to be in alliance with evil spirits and treated with a mixture of fear and respect. Curious and creative minds often *were* interested in the occult, for no line could be drawn between science and superstition, and an advanced case, like the famous Dr John Dee, could be the cause of trouble.

Dee was interested in many matters and undoubtedly did have more than a trace of Faust about him. He was forced to leave England in 1548, fresh out of Cambridge University, on suspicion of being a "conjuror". He was in trouble again in the reign of Mary, accused of enchantments and briefly imprisoned. But in 1558 he was asked

to recommend an auspicious day for Elizabeth's coronation and he subsequently became the Queen's astrologer and adviser on mystical matters: Elizabeth was always promising him great rewards, though they never materialized. In 1578 Dee went to Germany to consult with German astrologers regarding an illness the Queen was suffering from, and in 1583 he went abroad for a longer spell, maintaining himself, apparently, on his reputation for calling up spirits. While he was absent, a mob broke into his house and destroyed his books, manuscripts and laboratory, as things tainted with evil.

It is difficult to tell how widespread and how sincere belief in the supernatural really was. It was certainly declining: "God in times past", wrote Reginald Scot in *The Discovery of Witchcraft* (1584), "did send down visible angels and appearances to men; but now he doth not so". The decline in credulity was not great, however. Did Shakespeare believe in ghosts? Probably. In witches? Probably not. But James I certainly did. In 1591 he was involved in a famous case of witchcraft in North Berwick, near Edinburgh, the circumstances of which were so exotic that James thought the alleged witches must be making everything up. But they, to prove their truthfulness,

described to him what had been said in the privacy of the bedchamber on the first night of his honeymoon, which the King admitted was perfectly accurate. He remained always extremely interested in the subject and discussed it at length with, among many others, Sir John Harrington, who recorded that James spoke "with much gravity". This suggests that Sir John took the matter somewhat less seriously than the King. However, alleged witches were persecuted, tortured and killed throughout the 17th century. The whole subject has aroused much interest among today's historians, who have shown that witchcraft, superstition and paganism were more significant in English society than had previously been realised.

Witches were commonly believed to be capable of flying through the air, of transfixing an enemy's liver with needles, of turning themselves or others into animals. Some of the most enlightened people believed such things, and to question the existence of witches was tantamount to heresy. Reginald Scot went no further than to query, not that witches existed, but "whether they can do such marvellous works as are imputed to them". Even that much scepticism incurred a reprimand from James I.

CONCLUSION

Golden ages, as the great British historian G.M. Trevelyan once remarked, are not all gold and usually last for much less than "an age". The Golden Age of Elizabethan England lasted hardly more than a couple of decades. Think of any of the more remarkable cultural achievements of the Elizabethan period and the great majority date from 1580 or later; the first half of the Queen's reign was comparatively uneventful, and by 1603 she was dead. Of course, her death in itself altered nothing. Shakespeare did not stop writing plays when the Queen died, in fact his major works belong mostly to the reign of James I; yet the disappearance of the presiding goddess takes most of the glitter out of the picture. Under the Stuarts subtle and on the whole unattractive changes can soon be discerned. Heroic tragedy declines towards melodrama; even the household furniture becomes somehow coarser.

In spite of the shadows—the very high rate of crime and unemployment for instance—and disregarding the inevitable injustice and cruelty of the age, it was a special moment in English history. England was still a place where city, village, farm and forest co-existed in reasonable balance. Industrialization had not begun to threaten the creative craftsman with redundancy, yet the throttling economic restrictions of the Middle Ages were fast disappearing. In other ways too minds were breaking away from rigid, long-established limits, and had not yet fallen under the spell of one or other equally restricting if more modern dogmatism. Knowledge was not yet specialised, and for all the superstition of the times, in some ways the world was much simpler and more comprehensible than it is now. Wonderful new possibilities were just beginning to appear, and the effect was stimulating.

Although by 1588 the country was at war, at home there was peace. At least, no marching armies disturbed the agricultural improvements of the countryside or the lively growth of the towns. Indeed, the Spanish war merely emphasised the new spirit of national pride and encouraged further those maritime exploits of discovery and commerce which were so significant a feature of the age.

It would be possible to list numerous factors that contributed to the uniqueness of the age, yet there remains a touch of magic about Elizabethan England which is not to be explained by the most comprehensive summary of social, economic or political circumstances, and is only, perhaps, to be sensed through the words of the poets.